Supporting people in their own homes

The Skills for Care common induction training standards for domiciliary care workers

Malcolm Day, Elaine Grade and Elaine Wilson

Pavilion

Supporting People in their Own Homes

The Skills for Care common induction training standards for domiciliary care workers

© Malcolm Day, Elaine Grade and Elaine Wilson

Published by:
Pavilion Publishing (Brighton) Ltd
Richmond House
Richmond Road
Brighton BN2 3RL
UK

Tel: 01273 623222
Fax: 01273 625526
Email: info@pavpub.com
Web: www.pavpub.com

First published 2008.

A Catalogue record for this book is available from the British Library.

ISBN: 978 1 84196 235 1

Pavilion is the leading training and development provider and publisher in the health, social care and allied fields, providing a range of innovative training solutions underpinned by sound research and professional values. We aim to put our customers first, through excellent customer service and good value.

Editor: Bonnie Craig, Pavilion
Cover design: Faye Thompson, Pavilion
Page layout and typesetting: Faye Thompson, Pavilion
Printed on paper from a sustainable resource by: Ashford Press.

Contents

Chapter three: Maintaining health and safety at work

Chapter four: Communicating effectively

Chapter five: Recognise and respond to abuse and neglect

Appendix one

Appendix two

Appendix three

List of activities

The aims and objectives of these training materials

When you have completed these training materials you will:

- be familiar with the fundamental principles of *domiciliary care* and know how these can be used to maintain the independence of service users with minimal risk

- be able to identify how your practice as a *domiciliary care worker* might be influenced by legislation, policies, procedures and relationships at work

- recognise how best practice at work can maintain the health, safety, security and well-being of colleagues and service users in the *domiciliary care environment*

- be able to indicate how the domiciliary care worker can communicate safely and effectively with colleagues, other professionals and service users

- be able to state how the domiciliary care worker might utilise policies and procedures to recognise, and then respond appropriately to, the potential abuse and neglect of people in their own homes

- be able to indicate how support and supervision in the workplace might contribute to the development of the skills and knowledge of the domiciliary care worker.

How to use these training materials

Throughout each chapter, the symbol ☺ is used to assist you with your learning. This symbol prompts you to undertake a learning activity.

At the end of each chapter you are prompted by the ♀ symbol to complete a knowledge test. These short tests are intended to evaluate your learning. They are not intended to catch you out in any way; rather, they give you an opportunity to review what you have learned and to revisit and/or revise key parts of the chapter.

At the end of each chapter you are also prompted by the ✍ symbol. This asks you and your supervisor or mentor to record that you have satisfactorily completed each of the learning activities contained in the chapter.

If you undertake all of the learning activities and the knowledge tests, and place them in a portfolio, you will be able to demonstrate that you have satisfactorily completed the *Common Induction Standards* (Skills for Care, 2005). You may also be able to gain credit for your learning, for example, towards a National Vocational Qualification (NVQ).

Please read **Introduction** on page 3 for further information.

About the authors

Malcolm Day is a Registered Nurse and Registered Nurse Teacher. He is a licentiate member of the Institute of Verifiers and Assessors, a fellow of the Institute for Learning and a fellow of the Higher Education Academy. He has worked as a Trainer for NVQs and Foundation and Advanced Apprenticeships in Health and Social Care. He was previously an external Verifier for NVQs in Health and Social Care and an external Examiner for HND/HNC in Early Years and Care. Malcolm has held university lectureships in nursing, community care and care management. He was a member of the Skills for Care Induction and Foundation Review Committee. He is author of *Caring for the Older Person*, published by Pavilion Publishing (Brighton) Ltd.

Elaine Grade is a Registered Nurse, a Member of the Institute for Conflict Management and a qualified NVQ Assessor and Verifier. She is also a qualified Manual Handling Facilitator. She has run her own domiciliary care agency and was previously a Senior Nurse Manager at a regional nursing agency. She has also worked as a Healthcare Trainer – delivering and writing training materials for care workers, specialist nurses and assistant healthcare practitioners. Elaine previously worked for Allied Healthcare as Head of Training. She currently works as Head of Recruitment and Training with Anchor Care.

Elaine Wilson is a Registered Nurse and a qualified NVQ Assessor and Verifier. She is also a member of the Institute for Learning, and a member of the Chartered Management Institute. Elaine has previously run her own domiciliary care agency. She has also worked as a Training Manager, Lead Trainer and NVQ Quality Co-ordinator in a further education college, and as an NVQ Co-ordinator at an NHS trust. Elaine currently works as a Specialist Training Manager for Allied Healthcare and is involved in the development of induction and mandatory training programmes.

Introduction

WHAT IS A DOMICILIARY CARE WORKER?

The Domiciliary Care Agencies Regulations defines a domiciliary care worker as a person who is employed by a service provider to give personal care to people in their own homes, particularly for persons who: *'by reason of illness, infirmity or disability are unable to provide it for themselves without assistance'* (The Stationery Office, 2002).

The Department of Health (DoH) paper *Supported Housing and Care Homes – Guidance on regulation* (2002a) defines personal care as providing the following functions.

1. Assistance with bodily functions such as feeding, bathing and toileting.

2. Care falling just short of assistance with bodily functions, but still involving physical and intimate touching, including activities such as helping a person to get out of a bath and helping them to get dressed.

3. Non-physical care, such as advice, encouragement and supervision, relating to the foregoing, such as prompting a person to take a bath and supervising them during this.

4. Emotional and psychological support, including the promotion of social functioning, behaviour management and assistance with cognitive functions.

In March 2008 domiciliary care workers were (for the first time) admitted to the Social Care Register. The Social Care Register is maintained by the General Social Care Council (GSCC), and is a register of people who work in social care who have been assessed as trained and fit to be in the social care workforce.

The GSCC is the workforce regulator and guardian of standards for the social care workforce in England. It was established in October 2001 under the Care Standards Act (2000).

TRAINING FOR DOMICILIARY CARE WORKERS

As a newly appointed domiciliary care worker, the GSCC will want to know that you can contribute in a safe and appropriate manner to the work carried out in a service user's home. Induction training is the way that your manager ensures that you can contribute to the quality of care that is provided, and that you do not make dangerous, or costly, mistakes that could put service users at risk. Induction can be a learning programme of important basic skills and knowledge that takes place over a short period of time *before* you begin your new job as a domiciliary care worker. Or it can be a thorough programme of learning that takes place under supervision *during* the first weeks of your new job. Whichever approach is used, your manager is best placed to make sure that your induction is carried out properly. In some larger organisations you may be inducted by a mentor – a more experienced domiciliary carer who will work alongside you, and guide you, during your induction. Your manager may also get some help from a trainer or a college for any specialist parts of your induction (for example, manual handling or fire awareness). The government states that your induction programme *must* be completed within the first 12 weeks of your employment and this is monitored by the Commission for Social Care Inspection (CSCI). It also states that your induction *must* be based on the *Common Induction Standards* (Skills for Care, 2005) and the *Code of Practice for Social Care Workers* (GSCC, 2002a).

SKILLS FOR CARE COMMON INDUCTION STANDARDS

The *Common Induction Standards* (Skills for Care, 2005) are a minimum standard for the induction of newly appointed staff in the social care sector. There are six common induction standards:

- Standard 1 Understand the principles of care

- Standard 2 Understand the organisation and the role of the worker

- Standard 3 Maintain safety at work

- Standard 4 Communicate effectively

- Standard 5 Recognise and respond to abuse and neglect

- Standard 6 Develop as a worker.

Each of these standards has a list of the main areas that you will need to understand. Each main area has a set of outcomes that describe what you must be able to do. Some of these units also cover parts of the NVQ in Health and Social Care. The NVQ is the next level of qualification that you will need to undertake, and care workers must have a Level 2 NVQ in Health and Social Care by March 2008.

GSCC CODE OF PRACTICE FOR SOCIAL CARE WORKERS

The *Code of Practice for Social Care Workers* (GSCC, 2002a) describes the standards of professional conduct and practice required of domiciliary care workers as they go about their daily work. As a domiciliary care worker, you must fulfil the following responsibilities.

1. Protect the rights and promote the interests of service users and carers.

2. Strive to establish and maintain the trust and confidence of service users and carers.

3. Promote the independence of service users while protecting them as far as possible from danger or harm.

4. Respect the rights of service users while seeking to ensure that their behaviour does not harm themselves or other people.

5. Uphold public trust and confidence in social care services.

6. Be accountable for the quality of your work and take responsibility for maintaining and improving your knowledge and skills.

This code reflects existing good practice and must be met by all social care workers. The common induction standards have been designed to help you meet the requirements of the *Code of Practice for Social Care Workers* (GSCC, 2002a).

GETTING STARTED ON YOUR INDUCTION PROGRAMME

Each unit of this training programme is based on the common induction standards and the *Code of Practice for Social Care Workers* (GSCC, 2002a). You and your manager can systematically work through the learning activities in order to achieve each of the standards. You might want to keep the written learning activities that you complete in a portfolio. This will help you later in your career, particularly if you want to undertake an NVQ. In fact, all the chapters in this manual are cross-referenced to the Level 2 NVQ in Health and Social Care.

WHAT IS A PORTFOLIO?

A portfolio is a permanent record of your learning, which is kept in a binder, file or folder. If you go for an interview or change jobs, it can be used to show that you have already completed the common induction standards. If you want to undertake further training (such as an NVQ), you can use your portfolio to show what you already know and can do, and it will enable you to gain credit for this – for example, through accreditation of prior learning (APL). Your portfolio will include any induction plans you agree with your manager, any written learning activities you complete and any evidence that might support your learning, such as specialist training certificates. Your portfolio should be organised logically and sequentially, with an index at the front showing how each of your learning activities, training certificates etc relate to each of the common induction standards. So, for example, the first section of your portfolio will be headed **Standard one: Understand the principles of care** and will contain the evidence of your learning activities in this topic area.

ACCREDITATION OF PRIOR LEARNING (APL)

At the end of your induction, you might want to submit your portfolio towards the relevant units of a Level 2 NVQ in Health and Social Care. If you intend to do this, you must ensure that all the learning recorded in your portfolio is your own work and that it can be verified by a senior colleague. This is why any record of your learning must be dated and countersigned by your mentor or supervisor (see, for example, *Activity 1: Plan of action*).

☺ Activity 1: Plan of action

Make an appointment with your manager to discuss your induction programme. Draw up an agreed plan of action that includes:

- when your induction programme will start and finish

- what your induction programme will cover

- who will deliver specialist aspects of the programme (eg. moving and handling)

- who will provide help and advice during your induction (eg. your mentor)

- how your learning will be assessed during and at the end of your induction

- how your induction programme will be evaluated by you and your manager.

The form opposite will help you and your manager to do this.

✍ Action plan for my induction

© Malcolm Day 2005

1. Name of domiciliary care worker ....

2. Name of manager ....

3. Name of employer ....

4. Induction start date ....

5. Expected induction completion date ....

6. The content of my programme will include the following common induction standards:

    Standard 1 Understand the principles of care
    Standard 2 Understand the organisation and the role of the worker
    Standard 3 Maintain safety at work
    Standard 4 Communicate effectively
    Standard 5 Recognise and respond to abuse and neglect
    Standard 6 Develop as a worker.

7. I will also undertake the following specialist training:

    ■ moving and handling
    ■ fire awareness and safety
    ■ food handling and hygiene
    ■ working safely with hazardous substances
    ■ others [please state] ....

8. My specialist training will involve some practical and written tests. It will be delivered by [please state] ....

9. During my induction I will be supported by a mentor. His/her name is

    ....

10. At the end of my induction I will have an appraisal with my manager. The purpose of the appraisal is for both of us to review how I have got on during my induction and for us to decide whether I need any further training or support.

Signed .... Date ....
(Domiciliary care worker)

Signed .... Date ....
(Manager)

Chapter one

Chapter one

The principles of caring

AIMS OF THIS CHAPTER
As described in the introduction to this book, there are nationally agreed common induction standards and codes of practice that underpin the way you work with service users and their families, other members of the care team and your managers. This chapter aims to guide you through the first of these standards:

Standard 1.0 Understand the principles of care
    1.1 The values
    1.2 Confidentiality
    1.3 Person-centred approaches
    1.4 Risk assessment.

This standard also relates to the following units of the Level 2 NVQ in Health and Social Care:

- **HSC21:** Communicate with and complete records for individuals
- **HSC22:** Support the health and safety of yourself and individuals
- **HSC23:** Develop your knowledge and practice
- **HSC24:** Ensure your own actions support the care, protection and well-being of individuals.

CARE VALUES
You and your mentor will discuss the care values and beliefs that underpin domiciliary care work. They are principles of good practice that aim to minimise prejudice and discrimination. You can demonstrate these by:

P   respecting **privacy**

R   respecting the **rights** of individuals

I   recognising **individuality**

C   working **collaboratively** with individuals and enabling them to make **choices**

I   encouraging **independence**

D   preserving **dignity**.

P R I C I D

☺ Activity 2: Care values (a)

Please read the following case study and then answer the questions that follow.

Mrs Elsie Smith, 79 years old, has been living in sheltered accommodation for five years. She is well liked by others in the neighbourhood. She has objected to a new neighbour using a shared pathway to the rear of the sheltered housing scheme. The pathway is located between Mrs Smith's and her new neighbour's bungalow. Mrs Smith tells you that she has been in her bungalow longer than 'he' has, and therefore has more right to use the pathway than he has. She also tells you that the new neighbour has had a stroke and that he 'wets himself'. She says he 'smells' and shouldn't be allowed to live on his own unsupervised.

1. Do you think that Mrs Smith is being prejudiced in any way? If so, please state why.

2. Do you think that Mrs Smith has discriminated against the new neighbour in any way? If so, please state why.

continued ⇨

☺ Activity 2: Care values (a) (continued)

3. Use this page to write short notes on how the care values (**P R I C I D**) might be used to ensure that the needs of Mrs Smith and her new neighbour are met.

MRS SMITH

Privacy

Rights

Individuality

Choices

Independence

Dignity

THE NEW NEIGHBOUR

Privacy

Rights

Individuality

Choices

Independence

Dignity

PREJUDICE, DISCRIMINATION AND EQUAL OPPORTUNITIES

Prejudices are the ideas and beliefs that we have about people and that may cause us to judge them before we get to know them properly. Prejudice is a human trait that is present in all of us. Prejudices are often shaped and influenced by our immediate social circle, for example, families, friends and work colleagues. Prejudices are often expressed as negative thoughts about other people's age, appearance, disability, gender, politics, race or religion.

This is not an exhaustive list. Almost any negative belief about others who exist outside our immediate social circle might be regarded as prejudice. Unfortunately these beliefs can sometimes be demonstrated through negative actions, when we are discriminating against others. Discrimination occurs when we treat others unfairly because of their appearance or beliefs. There are laws that aim to minimise the effects of discrimination and promote equal opportunities. These include:

- the Equal Pay Act (1970) – men and women doing work of equal value should be paid the same

- the Sex Discrimination Act (1975) – men and women have equal rights to employment, services and facilities

- the Race Relations Act (1976) – all forms of racial discrimination are prohibited

- the Disability Discrimination Act (1995) – a disabled person must not be treated less favourably than someone who is able bodied.

☺ Activity 3: Care values (b)

Arrange some time with your mentor to discuss the following issues.

1. What beliefs do people generally have about a disabled person?
2. How might these beliefs be demonstrated as a form of discrimination?
3. How could you, as a domiciliary care worker, promote equality for disabled people?

Record what you have learned below.

1. Beliefs that people might have about a disabled person

2. Possible forms of discrimination or prejudice

3. Promoting equality

CONFIDENTIALITY

Service users trust you to maintain their dignity and privacy, and expect you to be discreet. Privacy and dignity are care values (remember **P R I C I D**?)

Everybody has a right to have their privacy respected. For example, how would you feel if details of your personal life were made common knowledge? You might feel let down, angry or distressed. Therefore, as a general rule, what you are told as a care worker must remain *confidential*. This might include:

■ financial affairs
■ medical conditions
■ mental health problems
■ personal beliefs
■ personal relationships
■ physical disabilities
■ sexual orientation
■ religious beliefs.

Personal information about service users is recorded in a number of ways:

■ care plans
■ case notes
■ medical records
■ observation charts
■ prescription charts.

Remember, you are in a privileged position to be able to access this information and it is your responsibility to ensure that it remains confidential. In doing so, you will be able to demonstrate to service users and colleagues that you are trustworthy.

Of course, there may be circumstances when confidentiality has to be broken, for example, if someone has broken the law or if another service user might be put at risk (see *Activity 4: Confidentiality (a)*).

☺ Activity 4: Confidentiality (a)

A service user with learning disabilities wants to confide in you about a personal matter that she thinks is very serious. However, she wants you to promise that you won't tell anyone what she says.

1. What should you say to her?
2. Who should you disclose information to, and under what circumstances?

Record your answers below.

1. What I should say

2. Whom I should disclose information to under these circumstances

You may receive requests for information about service users. Before you give out any information make sure you do the following things.

1. Have permission to do so.
2. Confirm the identity of the enquirer.
3. If it is a telephone request – ask for their phone number and call them back.

Similarly, if a passer-by asks to visit a service user, you should first confirm their identity and then check with the service user that they would like to see the visitor.

You must never give out any information unless the service user has given their consent (see **Activity 5: Confidentiality (b)**).

☺ Activity 5: Confidentiality (b)

You receive a phone call from a young man who says he is the boyfriend of a work colleague. He asks when your colleague is finishing her shift, so that he can pick her up.

1. What would you do?
2. What is your organisation's policy on the disclosure of personal information?

Record your answers below.

1. What I would do

2. The organisation's policy on confidentiality and disclosure of information

PERSON-CENTRED APPROACHES

A service provider is an organisation that provides people with services. For example, your borough council provides you with schools and libraries etc. You use the services provided by the borough council, therefore you are a service user. You work for an organisation that provides domiciliary care – it is a care service provider. The clients you care for in their own home are care service users.

Groups of care service users will have similar needs. For example, within domiciliary care, older infirmed people are the predominant care service user group (although they are not the only care service user group). Older infirmed people might suffer from a particular health condition, such as a stroke. They might have temporary confusion or dementia. They might have a mental health problem, such as depression. They might have a physical disability or sensory impairment, such as loss of hearing or loss of sight.

Think back to *Activity 3: Care values (b)*. How do you think people view the older disabled person? For example, how many times have you heard people raise their voice to an older person because they believe that most older people are deaf? How often do you hear people express surprise when an older person says they enjoy an active sex life? How many times have you been surprised when an older person has achieved an Open University degree, or has just completed the London marathon? The general assumption is that once an individual has retired from paid employment, they can no longer actively contribute to the community. However, older people are important role models for younger people, because they can demonstrate the positive benefits of becoming older.

☺ Activity 6: Person-centred approaches (a)

What, in your view, are the positive benefits of becoming older? Does the older person become wiser? Does the older person have more patience? If so, how might these attributes be put to good use in the family, in your neighbourhood or in society as a whole?

Record your answers below.

Whether your service user is physically infirmed, or has a learning disability or a chronic mental health disability, it is most important that you have a positive approach towards their care. You can do this by:

- encouraging them to be independent and make their own decisions
- respecting them as individuals and not behaving in a discriminatory way
- ensuring you respect the confidentiality of any information that they give you
- encouraging them to participate in their own care planning.

Care planning involves the systematic assessment and recording of individual needs in the service user's care plan. It follows the following cycle.

1. **Assessment:** asking about service user needs and obtaining a history of care, discussing goals and agreeing on the care needed.

2. **Implementation:** encouraging independence and providing support as agreed.

3. **Monitoring:** asking individuals about the outcomes of their care and giving feedback to the care team.

4. **Evaluation:** obtaining feedback on the care that has been delivered and negotiating and agreeing new goals with the service user.

Therefore, the care plan should contain the following information:

- the individual's particular care needs or problems
- the rationale or main reasons for providing care
- the goals that the care activities are designed to achieve
- the care activities that are being provided in order to achieve the goals
- the agreed timescales for achieving the goals, including a review date
- how the care plan is to be reviewed and updated to ensure that the goals have been achieved.

Care Homes for Older People National Minimum Standards (DoH, 2002b) states that an initial assessment of care needs should include:

- personal care and physical well-being
- diet and weight, including dietary preferences
- sight, hearing and communication
- oral health
- foot care
- skin care
- mobility and dexterity
- history of falls
- continence
- medication usage
- mental state and cognition
- social interests, hobbies and religious and cultural needs

- personal safety and risk
- carer and family involvement and other social contacts/relationships.

The following learning activities are designed to assist you in assessing the care needs of a service user.

☺ Activity 7: Person-centred approaches (b)

Think about two service users with whom you have recently worked. What individual characteristics do they have, with regard to their health status and physical, mental, sensory and social ability? You will need to make a copy of this sheet so you can complete a separate one for each service user.

Initials of service user

Health status

Physical ability

Mental ability

Sensory ability

Social ability

NB If at any time you notice change in a service user's health status or physical, mental, sensory or social ability, you **must** discuss this with your supervisor and record it in the service user's care plan.

PERSONAL HYGIENE

Some of your service users will have personal care needs. For example, they might need help in maintaining their personal hygiene because of a long-term physical disability, such as a stroke. They might be acutely ill – a bout of flu, for example – and need a temporary rest in bed. They might be confused or disorientated or depressed and need some supervision or assistance with personal hygiene. Why is this care activity so important?

☺ Activity 8: Person-centred approaches (c)

Think about the ways in which the inability to maintain personal hygiene might affect the daily lives of the service users with whom you work. Discuss this with your mentor and then complete the following table.

Poor hygiene	Effects on daily living
Anal region	
Clothing	
Feet	
Genital region	
Hands and nails	
Hair	
Mouth and teeth	

NB If at any time you notice change in a service user's ability to maintain their own personal hygiene, you **must** discuss this with your supervisor and record it in the service user's care plan.

EATING AND DRINKING

Many of your service users will need help with eating and drinking. They might not be physically capable of feeding themselves because of a disability. They might be confused or disorientated and might not recognise the need to eat or drink. They might have temporarily lost their appetite because of the effects of an acute illness, ill-fitting dentures or medication. Why is this care activity so important?

☺ Activity 9: Person-centred approaches (d)

Think about the ways in which the inability to eat or drink might affect the daily lives of the service users with whom you work. Discuss this with your mentor and then complete the following table.

Reduced intake	Effects on daily living
Carbohydrates	
Fats	
Fluids	
Proteins	
Vitamins	

NB If at any time you notice change in a service user's ability to eat or drink, you **must** discuss this with your supervisor and record it in the service user's care plan.

ELIMINATION

A number of your service users might need help with using the toilet. They might have mobility problems that make it difficult to walk to the toilet. They might also be suffering from 'urgency' – an overwhelming and uncontrollable desire to void urine because of weakness of the muscles in and around the bladder. This condition may lead to 'leakage' and can be very distressing. Why is this care activity so important?

☺ Activity 10: Person-centred approaches (e)

Think about the ways in which urinary urgency might affect the daily lives of the service users with whom you work. Discuss this with your mentor and then complete the following table.

	Effects on daily living
Independence	
Social contact	
Self-image	
Personal hygiene	
Skin	
Diet	

NB If at any time you notice change in a service user's ability to use the toilet, you **must** discuss this with your supervisor and record it in the service user's care plan.

MOBILITY

Many of the service users with whom you work will also need help with their mobility. They might have become permanently incapacitated because of the effects of a long-term disability, such as a stroke or chronic chest disease. They might be temporarily incapacitated because of the effects of an acute illness, such as a chest infection. Why is this care activity so important?

☺ Activity 11: Person-centred approaches (f)

Think about the ways in which immobility might affect the daily lives of the service users with whom you work. Discuss this with your mentor and then complete the following table.

	Effects on daily living
Activity	
Diet	
Independence	
Elimination	
Muscles and joints	
Skin	
Social life	

NB If at any time you notice change in a service user's mobility, you **must** discuss this with your supervisor and record it in the service user's care plan.

MOBILITY AND PRESSURE SORES

A pressure sore is an area of the skin in which the blood supply is cut off and, as a result, the skin dies. In severe cases, the tissue underneath may be exposed. Service users are at risk from pressure sores if they are confused, depressed or disorientated, or have difficulty with:

- eating and drinking
- elimination
- mobility
- personal hygiene.

A pressure sore is caused by:

- chemicals found in urine and faeces, which can break down the surface of the skin
- friction, as the person slips or slides down the bed, or is dragged up or down the bed
- pressure on the skin, for example from hard parts of a bed or chair.

☺ Activity 12: Risk assessment

Think about the causes of pressure sores. Discuss with your mentor how these might be avoided.

Causes	How can these be avoided?
Urine and faeces	
Friction	
Pressure	

Find out about your organisation's policy on relieving pressure and managing pressure sores, and discuss this with your mentor.

RISK ASSESSMENT

Although it is important to maintain the dignity and independence of service users who are living in their own home, there can be occasions when the risk of injury to themselves or others might outweigh the benefits of undertaking this type of approach. For example, some service users may be confused and disorientated, therefore they may need supervision with their medication in order to minimise the risk of taking an overdose.

Risk assessments are undertaken by a trained, qualified person at the same time as the care plan is drawn up or revised. Risk assessments list the possible benefits of taking the risk against the possible adverse outcomes, the precautions that should be taken and the arrangements for reconsidering the matter, when appropriate. These factors, together with the conclusion of the risk assessment, will be recorded in the care plan. The responsibility of domiciliary care staff in relation to any risk likely to be faced by the service user will also be clarified. Risk assessments are reviewed at regular intervals, whenever circumstances change significantly or whenever a new risk arises.

The assessment of need will take into account all sources of possible risk. These might include the service user's own behaviour, illnesses or disabilities. For example, one way of determining whether a service user might be at risk of developing a pressure sore is to conduct a risk assessment using the Waterlow Scale. The Waterlow Scale assesses the risk of skin breaking down by examining different aspects of a service user's life, such as weight, continence, skin type, mobility, sex, age, appetite, health status and any medications they are taking. This produces a numerical score that indicates whether the service user has a low, high or very high risk of developing pressure sores.

However, a risk assessment might also include an assessment of the living environment, specifically dangerous items including medicines, the actions of other people who are regularly or occasionally present in the home, and situations arising if and when a service user leaves their own home.

The organisation's capacity to react to some of these sources of risk will be recognised and taken into account in the care plan, but it might, with the service user's permission, be possible to alert other people or agencies who can provide advice or take appropriate action to minimise the danger. For example, advice on pressure sores might be available from the tissue viability nurse and the nurse nutritionist.

WHAT HAVE I LEARNED ABOUT THE PRINCIPLES OF CARING?

So far, you have learned that the main service user is likely to be an older person, and that he or she could be suffering from a particular health condition, such as a stroke, respiratory disease or heart disease.

You have learned that the service user could have some form of temporary confusion or dementia, that they could have a mental health problem (such as depression) and that they could have a physical disability. They may also have some form of sensory impairment (such as loss of hearing or diminished sight).

You have also learned that it is very important that you take a positive approach towards service users by:

- respecting them as individuals
- encouraging them to be independent and to make their own decisions
- ensuring the confidentiality of any information they discuss with you
- encouraging them to participate in care planning.

Finally, you have learned that the service user might need assistance with their daily living activities in order to maintain an independent and healthy lifestyle.

The following activity is a case study intended to 'test' your learning. It is not intended to catch you out in any way; rather, it gives you and your mentor an opportunity to discuss and find out where your particular strengths lie, and where you might need some additional help or support.

☺ Activity 13: Person-centred approaches and risk assessment

Elsie Smith is 85 years old and has been living alone in her own home for five years. Elsie is permanently disabled and has restricted use of her right arm and right leg. Recently, Elsie has developed flu. She is unable to get out of bed, has a high temperature and is very lethargic. She has lost her appetite and is refusing to take her prescribed medication.

What are the immediate goals for Elsie's care?

How would you ensure that Elsie's daily living activities are maintained?

How might Elsie's risk of developing pressure sores be assessed?

How would you monitor the care that Elsie is receiving?

How will Elsie's care be recorded in her care plan?

Discuss your answers with your mentor.

💡 Test your knowledge

THE PRINCIPLES OF CARING
The following questions are intended to 'test' your learning. They are not intended to catch you out in any way; rather, they give you an opportunity to review what you have learned, and to revisit and/or revise key parts of this chapter.

1. What is meant by **P R I C I D**?

2. What is prejudice?

3. What is discrimination?

4. List three anti-discrimination laws.

5. List three ways in which confidential information about service users is recorded.

6. What are the four stages of care planning?

7. What is urinary urgency?

8. What effect can immobility have on muscles and joints?

9. List three causes of pressure sores.

10. How can the risk of pressure sore development be assessed?

Please refer to the answers in **Appendix one** (p115).

CONGRATULATIONS!
You have now completed the first chapter. Please ensure that you and your mentor complete the induction record on the next page, and that you place the answers to the learning activities in your **portfolio**.

When the induction record has been completed, place it in your **portfolio**, together with your **induction plan** and the answers to each of the **learning activities** you have completed.

✍ My induction record

© Malcolm Day 2005

1. Name of domiciliary care worker ....

2. Name of manager/supervisor ....

3. Name of employer ....

4. Induction start date ....

5. Expected date of induction completion ....

6. This is to confirm that .... (name of care worker)
   has satisfactorily completed all of the learning activities related to:

Standard 1.0 Understand the principles of care
   1.1 The values
   1.2 Confidentiality
   1.3 Person-centred approaches
   1.4 Risk assessment.

7. Any comments from care worker/supervisor or mentor?

Signed (domiciliary care worker): .... Date: ....

Signed (supervisor/mentor): .... Date: ....

Chapter two

The role of the worker

Chapter two

The role of the worker

AIMS OF THIS CHAPTER

This chapter builds on what you learned in **Chapter one**. It examines how the principles of care form the values and beliefs that are central to your role as a community care worker and how they influence the job you do. It also examines how your employer organises your workplace to ensure that these values and beliefs are maintained. When you have completed the activities contained in this chapter, you will have achieved the following standards:

Standard 2.0 Understand the organisation and the role of the worker
    2.1 Your role as a worker
    2.1 Policies and procedures
    2.3 Worker relationships

Standard 6.0 Develop as a worker
    6.1 Support and supervision
    6.2 Knowledge and skill development.

These standards also relate to the following units of the new Level 2 NVQ in Health and Social Care:

- **HSC21:** Communicate with and complete records for individuals
- **HSC22:** Support the health and safety of yourself and individuals
- **HSC23:** Develop your knowledge and practice
- **HSC24:** Ensure your own actions support the care, protection and well-being of individuals.

YOUR ROLE AS A CARE WORKER

Your role in the community involves many activities, including:

- building relationships with service users and their families
- assisting service users with personal care, such as washing and dressing
- providing social and emotional support
- getting to know service users' needs, hobbies and special interests.
- supporting service users to eat and drink
- supporting service users with shopping and laundry.

The specific requirements of your job will have been discussed at your interview. These will form part of your job description and contract of employment. The way in which you carry out these activities is determined by the care values (remember **P R I C I D**?). Your employer will ensure that these values are written down for service users and their families, so that they fully understand how care is provided in the care home. In addition, as a social care worker you are also required to comply with the *Code of Practice for Social Care Workers* (GSCC, 2002a), which states that you must fulfil the following responsibilities.

1. Protect the rights and promote the interests of service users and carers.

2. Strive to establish and maintain the trust and confidence of service users and carers.

3. Promote the independence of service users while protecting them as far as possible from danger or harm.

4. Respect the rights of service users while seeking to ensure that their behaviour does not harm themselves or other people.

5. Uphold public trust and confidence in social care services.

6. Be accountable for the quality of your work and take responsibility for maintaining and improving your knowledge and skills.

☺ Activity 14: Your role as a worker (a)

Obtain a copy of the *Code of Practice for Social Care Workers* (GSCC, 2002a) from www.gscc.org.uk and discuss with your mentor how the values it contains influence what you do in relation to the following parts of your work.

1. Assisting the service user with their personal hygiene.

2. Assisting the service user to dress.

3. Assisting the service user to eat and drink.

THE CARE TEAM

Many people make up the care team, these may include team leaders, senior carers or co-ordinators and members of the:

- administration team (eg. administrators, accounts and pay clerks)
- healthcare team (eg. doctors, district nurses and physiotherapists)
- social care team (eg. social workers, occupational therapists and priests).

Each individual is dependent on each other for the smooth running of the care package, and it is important that you know what each of them does, and the limitations that apply to their job. For example, imagine it is a service user's birthday. You might want to ask the office if it is possible to send a birthday card or other workers if they would like to contribute to buying some flowers. Each of these members of the care team will have a role in ensuring that the service user has a memorable birthday.

☺ Activity 15: Your role as a worker (b)

Think of an individual you have recently cared for. Identify the members of the care team who worked with you, and what their role was. List the initials of the team member and their role.

Initials	Role
1.	
2.	
3.	
4.	
5.	

Discuss this activity with your manager, to check that your answers are correct.

GETTING HELP TO DO YOUR JOB

From time to time, it is quite likely that you will require information or advice about your role as a care worker. You might want some information about your pay and conditions of service or future training, or you may feel that you are being harassed at work. There are a number of documents, individuals and organisations (for example, CSCI, your manager, trainer or trade union) that will provide the advice and information you might need. Look at *Activity 16: Your role as a worker (c)* and try to identify where the appropriate information and advice might be found. Discuss your answers with your mentor, to check that you have answered the questions correctly.

☺ Activity 16: Your role as a worker (c)

1. Where would you find information concerning the following issues?

■   Your rights as an employee

■   How domiciliary care is regulated

■   The training courses available to you

■   Harassment or bullying in the workplace

2. Who might you approach about the following issues?

■   Your rights as an employee

■   How domiciliary agency homes are regulated

■   The training courses available to you

WORKING WITH SERVICE USERS AND THEIR FAMILIES

You will be working very closely with the service user's family. This is important as involving the family will ensure that you meet the service user's need for love, self-esteem and security. It will also give you a better idea of the service user's likes and dislikes, frustrations, personal habits, hobbies and interests. This information will enable you to plan a more individualised approach to care. It will also ensure that the service user's independence is maintained. Finally, if you involve the family it will be possible to identify any behaviour that might be potentially neglectful or abusive. There are many ways in which you can involve the family. For example, you can involve them in:

- planning and reviewing the care of the service user
- assisting the service user with their personal care
- participating in social activities in the community
- participating in service user meetings in the community.

There are no hard or fast rules to involving the family. In fact, you can only be limited by your own imagination and creativity – but remember **P R I C I D**!

☺ Activity 17: Your role as a worker (d)

Before your next staff meeting, ask your manager if you can raise the issue of working with service users and their families.

1. During the meeting, lead a discussion on the various ways in which your care team might work more closely with service users and their families.

2. Make sure the team's ideas are recorded in the minutes of the meeting and then place a copy of these minutes in your portfolio.

3. Ask your manager to sign the minutes as confirmation of your role in leading and recording the outcomes of the discussion.

4. Did this activity result in any change to the employer's policy? Please give an explanation below.

ACCESS TO WORKPLACE POLICIES AND PROCEDURES

A policy is an official document that gives information about what must be done in your care home. It sets out the standards that you must achieve in your work, and gives a clear indication of your responsibilities in relation to them. Your employer will have many policies. For example, there will be a manual handling policy that outlines the health and safety laws and regulations with which, legally, you have to comply. This will include information about the standards for safe working practice with regard to manual handling – for example, the need to undertake a risk assessment before moving a heavy load.

A procedure is a document that explains how you should do your job, ie. it translates policies into working practice. Procedures are based on workplace values and principles to ensure that the job is done properly. For example, a manual handling procedure will tell you exactly how to undertake a risk assessment, covering all the stages in the process. It is very important that you follow the policies and procedures in your care home. In doing so, you will be:

- encouraging good practice
- maintaining the health and safety of staff, service users and their families
- obeying the law.

☺ Activity 18: Policies and procedures

One of your colleagues has suffered a needle stick injury.

1. Where would you find the policy that contains information on standards of safety relating to a needle stick injury?

2. Where would you find the procedure that tells you how to deal with a needle stick injury?

3. Why is it so important for you to follow this procedure exactly?

Record your answers below.

Where the policy can be found

Where the procedure can be found

Why it is important to follow this procedure

APPLICATION OF WORKPLACE POLICIES AND PROCEDURES

Remember, you are legally responsible for ensuring that the policies and procedures in your workplace are followed correctly. You are required to do so by a number of laws and regulations that govern practice in the workplace. They include:

- the Health and Safety at Work Act (1974)

- *The Health and Safety (First Aid) Regulations* (1981)

- the Data Protection Act (1998)

- the Food Safety Act (1990)

- *The Fire Precautions (Workplace) Regulations* (1997)

- *The Manual Handling Operations Regulations* (1992)

- human rights acts and anti-discrimination legislation

- *Control of Substances Hazardous to Health Regulations* (COSHH) (2002)

- *Reporting of Injuries, Diseases and Dangerous Occurrences Regulations* (RIDDOR) (1995).

Activity 19: Your role as a worker (e) looks at these acts and regulations and how they might influence your working practice. The first question has been completed to guide you.

☺ Activity 19: Your role as a worker (e)

How might each of the laws below influence your role at work?

Health and Safety at Work Act (1974)

Everyone has a legal responsibility to ensure that the workplace is free from any health and safety risk. Everyone has a right to information and training about health and safety.

The Health and Safety (First Aid) Regulations (1981)

Data Protection Act (1998)

Food Safety Act (1990)

The Fire Precautions (Workplace) Regulations (1997)

The Manual Handling Operations Regulations (1992)

Human rights and anti-discrimination acts

Control of Substances Hazardous to Health Regulations (COSHH) (2002)

Reporting of Injuries, Diseases and Dangerous Occurrences Regulations (RIDDOR) (1995)

WORKING RELATIONSHIPS

Think about the people you know and interact with every day (such as family, neighbours and colleagues at work). Your relationships with these individuals will include:

- family relationships (eg. with your parents, brothers or sisters)
- friendships (eg. with neighbours, work colleagues, former school friends)
- loving relationships (eg. with your child)
- sexual relationships (eg. with your partner, husband/wife or lover).

☺ Activity 20: Working relationships (a)

Think about the relationship you have with your doctor, your children or a friend. Would you say these are informal or formal relationships? What expectations do you have of each other? What roles does each of you play in the relationship?

Record your answers below.

Expectations in your informal relationships (eg. with family or friends)

Expectations in your formal relationships (eg. with your doctor)

Roles in your informal relationships (eg. with friends or family)

Roles in your formal relationships (eg. with your doctor)

Each of these relationships is well defined in our society and each individual will have clear expectations of each other. For example, sexual relationships are based on people being mutually consenting adults. Your relationship with a service user is based on the belief that you can be trusted to do no harm. This belief defines your role as a worker. As a care worker, you will be allowed to undertake intimate and personal activities, but only if the service user agrees. Therefore, your role as a caregiver is a formal one. It is based on consent. It is an agreement between you and the service user that is based on the care values discussed (remember **P R I C I D**?)

Occasionally you might observe inappropriate relationships. You are responsible for reporting this. Remember, the service user trusts you to do no harm, and to ignore inappropriate or abusive behaviour would be a breach of this trust. You should be particularly concerned if a service user has any unexplained:

- injuries (eg. cuts, bruises, burns)
- changes in behaviour (eg. crying, fearful, wanting to be alone)
- changes in condition (eg. loss of appetite, poor hygiene, weight loss)
- loss of money or belongings.

Sometimes, there will be a perfectly reasonable explanation for what has happened. However, if you are in doubt you should always report your concerns to your team leader or manager. Remember, the purpose of reporting your concerns is to protect people, including your co-workers, from potential abuse. No one will think any less of you for talking through your worries or concerns with your manager.

EFFECTS OF THE CARE SETTING ON THE WORKER AND THE CARE TEAM

Earlier in this chapter you examined the roles and responsibilities of different workers towards the service user. This section looks at the responsibilities that you and the care team have towards each other. The common goal of the care team is to care for, and provide support for, the people in their care. To be effective in achieving this goal, each member of the team has to be professional, reliable, trustworthy and respectful towards each other. Relationships in the team can sometimes be difficult, particularly as friendships change or develop. However, it is important for you to realise that any change in relationships can be observed or sensed by the service user, and may directly or indirectly influence the standard of care they receive. Of course, you don't have to be friends to work with other members of your team, but you are obliged to be helpful and courteous, and you are responsible for providing information that could:

- improve the way in which your team works
- improve the way in which individual members of your team work
- be used to solve any problems your team is having with their work
- be used to organise the daily workload of your team.

Team meetings are the best way to share this information – time set aside for you and your team to discuss things in a calm and rational manner. *Domiciliary Care: National minimum standards – regulations* (DoH, 2003) requires a meeting at least quarterly.

During team meetings, any feedback you give to others should be clear, helpful and constructive. You might say: *'I've noticed that... however, I have found it quicker if... What do you think? Shall we give it a try and see how it goes?'*

You should offer to take positive action in response to any constructive feedback you receive from the team. This will assist the team to grow and develop. You might say: *'I see what you are saying, you think it might be quicker if I... Ok, let's give it a try.'*

However, you should accept and respect differences of opinion, in order to avoid any personal conflict. You might say: *'I accept what you are saying, but I think we might have to agree to disagree on this issue.'*

When communicating with other members of the care team, you should use language appropriate to the care setting, and avoid any words, body language or humour that might be regarded (by others) as offensive.

☺ Activity 21: Working relationships (b)

Think about the way in which your team communicates and works with each other.

Identify one aspect that could be improved

How would you set about doing this?

Discuss your answers with your mentor.

SUPPORT AND SUPERVISION IN THE WORKPLACE

Work in the care sector can be extremely stressful, both in the conditions of service and in the nature of the work, and can occasionally be distressing. Caring in the community can also be lonely as you are usually working on your own. Symptoms of stress among care workers may include high levels of absenteeism, lack of concentration and illnesses such as headaches. Supervision is an effective way of improving standards, of reducing risks and of combating poor performance and stress. According to the *Domiciliary Care: National minimum standards – regulations* (DoH, 2003), care workers should receive formal supervision at least every three months and at least one of these sessions should take the form of direct observation of the worker providing care to a service user who they regularly work with. This should cover:

■ all aspects of care practice
■ the philosophy of care in the community
■ the career development needs of care workers.

While you are working in the community, you will be offered guidance and supervision from your manager and other experienced staff. The arrangements for this are both formal and informal.

Formal supervision is provided by your manager or team leader, who will conduct an appraisal of your performance at agreed times, according to the employer's staff development policy.

Appraisal is a mechanism that allows you and your manager to discuss, openly and frankly, any issues relating to your performance at work. It is not part of the disciplinary process; rather, it gives you and your manager an opportunity to identify the things that you are good at, and where you might benefit from further training and support. For example, you will have an appraisal at the end of your induction programme, during which you and your manager will review your performance against the Skills for Care standards. Your portfolio will provide a basis for this review.

While you are undertaking your induction programme you will also be guided, informally and continuously, by your manager or team leader. You may also be allocated a mentor. Mentorship is an informal arrangement and is usually provided by an experienced and trusted person from the care team, who is not part of the formal supervisory process. Mentorship is often provided by a senior care worker, who will offer you continuous advice and support. For example, your mentor could assist you with the activities in this training manual. Your manager and mentor have already been identified in your induction plan.

KNOWLEDGE AND SKILLS DEVELOPMENT

As indicated in the introduction to this book, the *Common Induction Standards* (Skills for Care, 2005) are a *minimum* standard for the induction of newly appointed staff in the care sector. Each of these standards directly relates to an NVQ in Health and Social Care at Level 2 or above. According to the *Domiciliary Care: National minimum standards – regulations* (DoH, 2003), at least half of care staff working with vulnerable adults will have achieved a Level 2 NVQ in Care. Also, your manager will probably have undertaken an NVQ Level 4 Registered Managers Award, or equivalent. The opportunities for personal and professional development in the care sector are many and varied. Skills for Care particularly emphasise the need for competence-based training via the many NVQs that exist within the health and social care sector.

WHAT IS AN NVQ?

An NVQ is an award that gives you credit for what you do in your job, every day. It is not like other qualifications that rely on taking a course or sitting a test or an examination, because you can use your performance on the job as a basis for assessment. If you are competent in your job, you will pass. NVQs are available at different levels. For example, the next level after your induction is Level 2. Your manager has probably undertaken a Level 4 NVQ, or its equivalent.

NVQs are made up of units, a bit like the units that make up your induction programme. These units specify the performance required of you to do your job. The units are made up of *mandatory* and *optional* units and you will need to achieve a combination of these in order to achieve your NVQ award. For example, an NVQ Level 2 is made up of the following units.

MANDATORY (FOUR UNITS AT LEVEL 2)
- **HSC21:** Communicate with, and complete records for individuals
- **HSC22:** Support the health and safety of yourself and individuals
- **HSC23:** Develop your knowledge and practice
- **HSC24:** Ensure your own actions support the care, protection and well-being of individuals

OPTIONAL (A CHOICE OF TWO UNITS AT LEVEL 2)
For example, you might choose the following optional units:

- **HSC214:** Help individuals to eat and drink
- **HSC215:** Help individuals to keep mobile

In order to register as an NVQ candidate you will need to contact an NVQ centre that is approved by an awarding body such as City & Guilds. In order to achieve your NVQ you will need to be assessed by an NVQ assessor from the approved centre. The NVQ assessor will assess you in your workplace. The work of the NVQ assessor is checked by an internal verifier, also from the approved centre. The work of the approved centre is checked by an external verifier, who is appointed by the awarding body.

Supporting People in their Own Homes © Pavilion Publishing (Brighton) Ltd 2008

APPRENTICESHIPS

Skills for Care is also encouraging care workers to undertake apprenticeships in health and social care. An apprenticeship is made up of three elements:

- an NVQ

- a technical certificate – this is a classroom-based award, generally taken on a day-release basis, which helps you to get to grips with the skills and knowledge that you need in the care professions

- a Key Skills award – this helps you to develop the skills you will need in employment (for example, communication, application of numbers, information technology, problem-solving, working with others and improving your own learning).

Apprenticeships are available at two levels: apprenticeship and advanced apprenticeship. At apprenticeship level, the technical certificate and NVQ are at Level 2. At advanced level, you work towards Level 3 awards.

More information on NVQs, apprenticeships and other types of training (such as administration of medicines, caring for older people with dementia etc) is available from Skills for Care at www.skillsforcare.org.uk

💡 Test your knowledge

THE ROLE OF THE WORKER

The following questions are intended to 'test' your learning. They are not intended to catch you out in any way; rather, they give you an opportunity to review what you have learned, and to revisit and/or revise key parts of this chapter.

1.   What is a policy?

2.   What is a procedure?

3.   What does COSHH stand for?

4.   What does RIDDOR stand for?

5.   What are the symptoms of stress at work?

6.   How often should workers receive formal supervision?

7.   What is appraisal?

8.   What is mentorship?

9.   What is an NVQ?

10. Give three reasons why it is important for you to follow the policies and procedures in your care home.

Please refer to the answers in **Appendix one** (p116).

You have now completed the second chapter. Please ensure that you and your mentor complete the induction record on the next page, and that you place the answers to the learning activities in your **portfolio**.

When the induction record has been completed, place it in your **portfolio**, together with your **induction plan** and the answers to each of the **learning activities** you have completed.

✍ My induction record

© Malcolm Day 2005

1. Name of domiciliary care worker ....

2. Name of manager/supervisor ....

3. Name of employer ....

4. Induction start date ....

5. Expected date of induction completion ....

6. This is to confirm that .... (name of care worker)
   has satisfactorily completed all of the learning activities related to:

Standard 2.0 Understand the organisation and the role of the worker
    2.1 Your role as a worker
    2.2 Policies and procedures
    2.3 Worker relationships

Standard 6.0 Develop as a worker
    6.1 Support and supervision
    6.2 Knowledge and skill development.

7. Any comments from care worker/supervisor or mentor?

Signed (domiciliary care worker): .... Date: ....

Signed (supervisor/mentor): .... Date: ....

Chapter three

Maintaining health and safety at work

Chapter three

Maintaining health and safety at work

AIMS OF THIS CHAPTER

This chapter will build on **Chapter two**, which examined your responsibility in relation to the legislation that covers health and safety at work. When you have completed this chapter, you will have achieved the following standards:

Standard 3.0 Maintain safety at work

    3.1 Health and safety
    3.2 Moving and handling
    3.3 Fire safety
    3.4 Emergency first aid
    3.5 Infection prevention and control
    3.6 Medication and healthcare procedures
    3.7 Security.

This unit also relates to the following units of the Level 2 NVQ in Health and Social Care:

- **HSC22:** Support the health and safety of yourself and individuals
- **HSC213:** Provide food and drink for individuals
- **HSC223:** Contribute to moving and handling individuals
- **HSC232:** Protect yourself from the risk of violence at work
- **HSC240:** Contribute to the identification of the risk of danger to individuals and others.

GENERAL HEALTH AND SAFETY

The Health and Safety at Work Act (1974) lays down the duties of employers and employees. Under this Act, the employer has to protect the health and safety of staff, service users and visitors, draw up safety policies and procedures, and make arrangements for the policies and procedures to be carried out. The employee has to ensure their own health and safety as well as the health and safety of others, and co-operate with their employer. The Health and Safety Executive (HSE) (2001) states that a general health and safety risk assessment should include the considerations listed overleaf.

FLOORS

- Are there slippery surfaces?
- Have spillages been cleaned up?
- Are floor surfaces suitable, flat, properly maintained?
- Are there obstructions or tripping hazards, such as rugs or frayed carpets?

STAIRS

- Are they well lit?
- Is the stair covering clean and in good condition?
- Are there obstructions?

LIGHTING

- Are bulbs working?
- Are lighting levels sufficient, including those on stairs and corridors?

VENTILATION

- Are there odours?
- Are there draughts?
- Is there sufficient fresh air?

WINDOWS

- Are security locks in place?
- Is glazing in good condition?
- Is the glazing material appropriate?

WATER AND SURFACE TEMPERATURES

- Are thermostatic mixing valves operating at the required temperature?
- Are radiators and pipes hotter than 43 degrees centigrade? If yes, what remedial action has been taken to protect vulnerable service users?
- Is the room temperature comfortable (ie. not too hot or cold)?

KITCHEN SAFETY

- Are floors clean, slip-resistant and dry?
- Is there room to move around safely?
- Is ventilation sufficient?
- Is food stored correctly, at the correct temperature?

OUTSIDE ENVIRONMENT

- Are steps and paths well lit and in good condition?
- Is there a well-lit parking area?
- Do workers have to pass through dark passageways to access the service user?
- Are workers aware of the company's lone worker policy?

ELECTRICAL APPLIANCES

- Are sockets, plugs and leads in good condition?
- Are sockets or adaptors overloaded?
- Do the electrical wires stop and start while in use or are they wrapped in tape?
- Is the equipment well maintained?

☺ Activity 22: Health and safety (a)

Use the list on the previous page to identify any potential hazards in your service user's home. Remember, you have a duty under health and safety legislation to report any potential hazards or any faults.

Record your answers below.

CONTROL OF SUBSTANCES HAZARDOUS TO HEALTH (COSHH)

There are many potentially hazardous substances and chemicals in your workplace, including:

- cleaning materials (eg. bleach and disinfectant) that can cause burns or poisoning
- drugs and medicines (eg. antibiotic powders) that can cause poisoning or allergic reactions
- latex (eg. protective gloves) that can cause skin allergies.

The *Control of Substances Hazardous to Health Regulations* (COSHH) (HSE, 2002) have been put in place to protect you against these harmful substances. In particular, COSHH states that employers must:

- ensure safe storage and disposal of substances that are harmful to health
- check that health hazards from all substances are assessed, including the laundry, kitchen and outdoors
- ensure appropriate control measures are implemented
- ensure staff are trained about safe procedures and use of protective clothing
- check that procedures for spillages are in place
- check that new staff are trained before using substances.

Before any substances are used in the workplace, employers must undertake the following risk assessment.

- What substances are present and in what form?
- What harmful effects are possible?
- Where and how are the substances stored, used and handled?
- Are harmful fumes produced, especially if products are mixed?
- Can a safer substance be used?
- Who could be affected, to what extent, for how long and under what circumstances?
- How likely is it that exposure will happen?
- Are precautions required, such as ventilation and protective equipment?

All substances under COSHH will tell you what protective clothing you should wear (if any), how to store any hazardous substances and how to dispose of any hazardous substances (for example, used needles should be placed in a yellow sharps box).

☺ Activity 23: Health and safety (b)

Think about substances in your service user's home that might be hazardous. Then complete the following table.

Substance	Precautions	Storage	Disposal
1			
2			
3			
4			
5			

You can use the safety labels from the various substances to complete this activity.

DEALING WITH AN ELECTRICAL OR GAS EMERGENCY

The Gas Safety (Installation and Use) Regulations (1998) apply to all gas appliances. All appliances, flues and pipework should be checked once a year by a registered CORGI engineer. Gas is flammable. It can cause explosions or fire. It can also cause asphyxiation. Your workplace will have a procedure for dealing with gas leaks but, as a rule, if there is a gas leak you should:

- ventilate the area by opening windows and doors to let the gas escape
- not light matches or cigarette lighters
- not touch any electrical switches
- turn off the gas at the mains
- use an external phone to call the gas emergency services
- give first aid if necessary, and dial 999 if an ambulance is needed (eg. for asphyxiation).

Electricity can also kill. It causes shock and burns and can also start fires. The use of electricity is covered by *The Electricity at Work Regulations* (1989). This includes lighting and power circuits, electrical equipment and appliances, such as washing machines, irons and vacuum cleaners. The main risk to people is contact with live parts causing shock and burns, for example, through frayed or exposed wiring. Your workplace will have a procedure for dealing with electrical emergencies but, as a rule, if one occurs, you should:

- turn off the power supply at the mains
- never touch a person or an object that is connected to the power supply
- give first aid if necessary, and dial 999 for an ambulance if needed (eg. for asphyxiation).

☺ Activity 24: Health and safety (c)

Find out where the main gas and electricity supplies in the service user's home can be turned off in an emergency and how to do this. Write short notes under the following headings and record these in the service user's plan.

The main gas shut-off valve is located at

The main electricity shut off switch is located at

The telephone number for a gas emergency is

The telephone number for an electrical emergency is

MOVING AND HANDLING

The spine is made up of 33 bones called vertebrae. These are joined together along the backbone in an S shape. The S shape gives our backbone flexibility and strength, and enables us to maintain our balance. If the spine is twisted out of shape, it can cause serious injury to the vertebrae. The spine protects our spinal cord. The spinal cord is a bundle of nerves that runs from the bottom of the spine to the brain. The spinal cord carries messages from the brain to the muscles and from the muscles to the brain. This enables us to maintain our posture and to move.

Damage to the spinal cord can cause paralysis. The vertebrae are cushioned by inter-vertebral discs. These act as shock absorbers. If too much pressure is put on these discs (eg. by lifting a heavy object) they can tear or prolapse. This can be very painful. The discs are linked together by spinal ligaments. If these become over-stretched (eg. by jerky or sudden movements), they can sprain and become swollen and painful. The muscles of the spine are the muscles of the back, chest and pelvis. They are attached to the vertebrae and give strength and flexibility to the spine. Strong and well-toned back muscles are essential for moving and handling activities. However, they can be easily torn and become swollen and painful.

☺ Activity 25: Moving and handling

1. On a piece of paper draw a diagram of the spine and label the following parts: cervical vertebrae; thoracic vertebrae; lumbar vertebrae; sacral vertebrae; the coccyx.

2. On a piece of paper, draw a diagram of lumbar vertebrae and label the following parts: inter-vertebral disc; inter-vertebral ligament.

3. Describe below how poor moving and handling techniques might injure your spine.

Check with your moving and handling trainer that your diagrams and answers are correct, then place them in the health and safety section of your portfolio.

The Manual Handling Regulations (1992) were introduced to reduce the number of injuries from moving and handling activities. The term 'manual handling' includes the lifting, moving, putting down, pushing, pulling and carrying by hand or bodily force of goods, equipment and people. An employer must avoid moving and handling where there is a risk of injury to staff, assess the risk of injury from moving and handling, and reduce the risk of moving and handling. An employee must make full and proper use of the manual handling systems and equipment provided.

You might be involved in moving objects as well as people. In order to reduce the risk of injury you should consider whether the move is necessary, whether it can be done in a different way, or whether any special equipment is needed. Your risk assessment should consider:

Task > Load > Environment > Individual capability.

TASK
You must assess whether the task involves:
- holding the load at a distance from your body
- bending, twisting, stooping or stretching
- moving the load over excessive distances
- frequent or prolonged physical effort
- any sudden movement of the load.

LOAD
You must assess whether the load is:
- heavy or bulky
- difficult to grasp
- unstable (eg. unpredictable behaviour)
- potentially harmful (eg. an agitated or aggressive individual).

ENVIRONMENT
You must assess whether:
- the space is adequate (eg. not restricted by furniture)
- the height is appropriate (eg. beds can be raised by wooden blocks)
- the floors are slippery or uneven
- the floors are level (eg. are there any slopes, stairs or frayed carpets?)

INDIVIDUAL CAPABILITY
You must consider yourself as well as other members of the team, particularly whether you or they:
- have been adequately trained in moving and handling
- are pregnant, or have a disability
- are wearing any clothing that might restrict their movement
- are wearing any jewellery that might injure any staff or service users
- are tired or fatigued.

All service users should have a risk assessment checklist within their care plan that you can use to generate an agreed plan.

Risk assessment checklist

- Is the individual weight-bearing? Yes/No

- Is the individual unsteady? Yes/No

- What is the individual's general level of mobility? Good/Poor

- What is the individual's weight? .... (Please state)

- What is the individual's height? .... (Please state)

- How many people are required to move this individual? .... (See care plan)

- What equipment is needed (eg. hoist, transfer board)? ....
.... (Please state)

- Is equipment available? Yes/No

- Is equipment clean? Yes/No

- If not, is there a safe alternative? Yes/No

....
.... (Please state)

- Is the required number of people available? Yes/No

- What is the purpose of the move? ....

....
.... (Please state)

- Can the move be safely achieved? Yes/No

As indicated in your induction plan, you will receive training from a specialist trainer in moving and handling techniques. However, as a general rule, you should always:

- undertake a risk assessment prior to any move
- follow the agreed lifting plan contained in the service user's notes
- give clear instructions to colleagues concerning the move
- check any equipment prior to its use
- ensure you maintain your centre of balance throughout the move
- hold the load close to your body, or get as close to the load as possible
- avoid bending, twisting, stooping or stretching
- avoid moving the load over excessive distances
- avoid frequent or prolonged physical effort
- avoid sudden movements
- allow adequate time for rest and recovery.

FIRE SAFETY

As indicated in your induction plan, you will receive training from a specialist trainer in fire awareness. Fire is a serious danger to vulnerable people and is responsible for many deaths. It can be prevented by:

- the use of smoke alarms
- ensuring all cigarettes are properly extinguished
- unplugging unused electrical equipment at night (eg. televisions)
- keeping fire doors closed to prevent the spread of fire
- ensuring that electrical and gas appliances have been properly checked for safety.

It is very important that you get to know your procedures for fire safety and that you attend fire training at least once a year. If you discover a fire you should:

- raise the alarm by using the fire alarm or dialling 999 for the fire brigade
- never enter the service user's home – if a fire is burning when you arrive ring the fire brigade and ambulance by dialling 999 and wait for them to arrive
- close windows and doors to prevent fire from spreading
- if the service user can move, escort them to a place of safety
- do not use any lifts, unless directed to do so by the fire brigade
- do not return to the building unless the fire brigade says it is safe to do so.

You might be able to put out a small fire by yourself, if it is safe to do so. For example, you could use a water-based fire extinguisher to put out a fire in wastepaper bin, or you might use a powder fire extinguisher to put out a small electrical fire in an office. You should not do this unless you are familiar with the various types of fire appliances. If used incorrectly, a fire appliance can cause serious injury or make the fire worse. For example, it is dangerous to use a water-based extinguisher on a chip-pan fire because it will cause the fire to 'flare up' and spread rapidly, and may cause severe burns to the person operating the extinguisher.

☺ Activity 26: Fire safety

Get to know how fire extinguishers are used by completing the following table.

Type of fire	Type of extinguisher to be used
Paper	
Electrical	
Petrol	
Cooking oil	

Discuss your answers with your fire training officer.

It is your responsibility to familiarise yourself with your employer's fire procedure. It is important that you recognise potential escape routes. Smoke alarms should be fitted in the homes of all vulnerable adults. For those with a hearing impairment, the smoke alarm may need to be a flashing light. It is important that you are informed of all adaptations.

EMERGENCY FIRST AID

Your role in giving emergency first aid is to:

- preserve a casualty's life
- prevent further harm
- promote or help their recovery.

You should only attempt to do this if you have undertaken a recognised emergency first aid course.

Reporting of Injuries, Diseases and Dangerous Occurrences Regulations (RIDDOR) (HSE, 1995) requires that any accident or injury that occurs at work, and the treatment given, must be recorded in your organisation's accident book.

As indicated in your induction plan, you will receive training in emergency first aid from a specialist trainer. During this training you will learn about the priorities in giving emergency first aid, ie:

D R A B

Danger: before you attempt any first aid, be sure that you are safe.

Response: is the casualty responding? Talk to them and place your mouth over each ear in case they are hard of hearing. If they respond, reassure them, and move them to a safer area if in danger.

Airway: if the casualty is unresponsive or unconscious, open the airway by gently tilting the casualty's head backwards and lifting their chin.

Breathing: Check the casualty is breathing normally. Put your cheek close to their mouth and look at their chest, place your hand on their chest, watch and listen for normal breathing for up to 10 seconds. If they are breathing normally but are unresponsive, put them in the recovery position (you will learn to do this on your first aid course). If they are not breathing, check that help is coming and then start resuscitation (you will learn to do this on your first aid course as well).

If your casualty has drowned, commence cardiopulmonary resuscitation (CPR) for one minute before going for help.

☺ Activity 27: Emergency first aid (a)

During your emergency first aid course you will be taught how to respond to different types of emergency. Please complete the following table (the first question has been completed to provide an example).

Type of emergency	Action
Minor wounds and bleeding	*Cover with sterile dressing. Apply pressure, and elevate. If bleeding continues, put another dressing on top of the first one and get help.*
Burns and scalds	
Choking	
Epileptic fit	
Fractures	

Discuss your answers with your Emergency first aid trainer.

USING PRIMARY HEALTHCARE SERVICES IN CASE OF ACCIDENT OR ILLNESS

Primary healthcare services are provided by the ambulance service, dentists, NHS Direct, general practitioners, nurses, pharmacists and physiotherapists. These are the professionals we first go to when we need advice if someone experiences an accident or ill health.

The ambulance service is an emergency medical service, staffed by trained paramedics. If a service user has an accident or a sudden life-threatening illness, such as a heart attack, you should telephone 999. You should clearly state:

- the casualty's name and age
- the location of the incident, address and telephone number
- any first aid already given.

The emergency operator will stay on the line and give you advice until the paramedics arrive.

NHS Direct is a national telephone advice line staffed by specially trained registered nurses. If a service user has a minor acute illness, such as flu, you can telephone NHS Direct for advice on 0845 4647.

General practitioners (GPs) are medical specialists in diagnosis, treatment and the referral of acute and chronic illnesses. If a service user becomes ill, you can contact the local GP or the deputising service and request a visit.

Many health authorities now provide NHS drop-in centres where a service user can be taken for advice or treatment of minor injuries or illnesses. These are usually staffed by emergency nurse practitioners.

Pharmacists can also provide over-the-counter advice for people with minor illnesses such as ear or eye infections. Some pharmacists, such as Boots, operate a 24-hour helpline.

Many physiotherapists will also provide emergency treatment for minor sports injuries or accidents at work, such as sprains or strains.

It is important that the service user maintains their registration with an NHS dentist, particularly if emergency treatment is required, as few health authorities now provide an out-of-hours dental service.

☺ Activity 28: Emergency first aid (b)

Note down where you can find details of the service user's GP, dentist and optician. Make a note of the NHS Direct telephone number and the nearest NHS drop-in centre.

Record your answers below.

GP

Dentist

Optician

NHS Direct

NHS drop-in centre

INFECTION CARE

Communicable or infectious diseases are caused by:

- bacteria (eg. food poisoning)
- viruses (eg. flu)
- fungi (eg. thrush).

The vulnerable adult is often at risk from infectious or communicable diseases because their immunity to micro-organisms, such as bacteria and viruses, is often low. This might be because of the medicines they are taking or their nutrition might be poor. Infection control, or the ways in which the spread of infection might be reduced, is an important part of a care worker's job. In fact, RIDDOR (HSE, 1995) requires that your employer reports certain cases of infectious diseases to the local environmental health officer.

Micro-organisms such as bacteria, viruses and fungi can be spread by:

- direct contact – being touched by an infectious person (eg. scabies)
- indirect contact – touching materials an infected person has used (eg. impetigo)
- inhalation – breathing in infected droplets from a cough or sneeze (eg. flu)
- ingestion – from contaminated food (eg. salmonella food poisoning)
- injection – from a needle stick injury (eg. HIV or hepatitis B).

Preventing the spread of blood-borne infections, such as HIV and hepatitis B, is a particularly important job for the care worker. In fact, you and your employer have a duty under COSHH to do this. The Health and Safety Executive (2001) indicates that the following is particularly important.

- The risk of contamination from infected materials, including used instruments, used needles and soiled laundry.

- Do you wear appropriate protective equipment and clothing?

- Do you cover cuts, grazes etc with waterproof dressings?

- Do you follow basic hygiene procedures, including regular hand-washing?

- Do you follow procedures for cleaning up spillages?

- Do you know how to deal with a needle stick accident? (Encourage bleeding, wash wound liberally with soap and water, report and record accident.)

- Have you been advised about hepatitis B immunisation?

 Supporting People in their Own Homes © Pavilion Publishing (Brighton) Ltd 2008

One of the most important measures you can take to prevent the spread of any infection is correct hand-washing technique, particularly before you:

- handle food
- give out any medicines
- give emergency first aid
- handle any wounds.

Also, you should wash your hands after you:

- use the lavatory
- assist others to use the lavatory
- cough, sneeze or use a handkerchief
- handle any dressings or wounds
- make beds
- handle rubbish
- handle raw food
- handle dirty or soiled laundry.

When washing your hands it is important that you use the following technique, as this will remove most of the bacteria that cause contagious diseases (that is, diseases spread by direct or indirect contact).

CORRECT HAND-WASHING TECHNIQUE

- Wet your hands with hot running water.
- Rub some liquid soap between your palms.
- Rub your right palm over the back of your left hand.
- Rub your left palm over the back of your right hand.
- Rub your palms together with your fingers interlocked.
- Rub the back of the fingers of your left hand with your right palm.
- Rub the back of the fingers of your right hand with your left palm.
- Rub around your left thumb with your right palm.
- Rub around your right thumb with your left palm.
- Rub your left fingertips round and round in your right palm.
- Rub your right fingertips round and round in your left palm.
- Rub your left wrist with your right hand.
- Rub your right wrist with your left hand.
- Rinse both hands thoroughly under running water.
- Dry each hand on a clean paper towel.
- Discard paper towel into pedal bin without touching the top or the sides of the bin.

Remember… the correct hand-washing procedure will take several minutes and you will still need to wash your hands even if you were wearing gloves.

☺ Activity 29: Infection control (a)

Ask a senior carer to carefully observe the hand-washing technique you are using. You could use the hand-washing checklist on the previous page to make sure you are using the correct procedure. Ask the senior carer to write a report on your hand-washing technique below.

SAFE FOOD HANDLING

Food that is not handled correctly can become contaminated with bacteria, viruses and fungi, which can cause food poisoning. The symptoms of food poisoning are nausea, vomiting, abdominal pain and diarrhoea. Food-poisoning bacteria grow in raw or waste food and rotting rubbish. Pests like mice and cockroaches carry food-poisoning bacteria. Food-poisoning bacteria are also carried by humans:

- Escherichia coli is found in faeces but is harmless until it is 'activated' by contact with food

- salmonella is found in raw meat, poultry, eggs, shellfish and faeces

- staphylococcus aureus is found on our skin, in our nose, throat, mouth, ears, hair and nails, and in cuts and boils.

RIDDOR (HSE, 1995) requires that your employer reports any cases of food poisoning to the local environmental health officer. Workplace procedures for safe food handling are governed by the Food Safety Act (1990) and *The Food Safety (General Food Hygiene) Regulations* (1995).

Good personal hygiene is particularly important for preventing the spread of food-poisoning bacteria. If you are involved in handling food, you should wash your hands with soap and hot running water before you handle food. You should also wash your hands after:

- handling any uncooked or waste food
- using the lavatory
- assisting service users to use the lavatory
- handling rubbish
- using or handling handkerchiefs or tissues
- coughing or sneezing
- touching your hair or face, or the hair or face of a service user.

If handling food, you should also:

- wear protective clothing
- keep your nails clean and short
- keep your hair tied back or covered
- cover any minor wounds with a coloured waterproof dressing
- not smoke in any area where food is being stored, prepared or served.

The spread of food-poisoning bacteria can also be controlled by cleaning and storing kitchen equipment correctly:

- separate plates or chopping boards should be used for preparing cooked and raw foods

- different equipment (knives, chopping boards, etc) should be used for raw and cooked foods, and kept separately

- work surfaces should be scrupulously cleaned after use for raw meat or poultry

- all food should be kept covered

- no food should be kept past its 'use-by' date.

The spread of food-poisoning bacteria can also be controlled by cooking and storing food at the correct temperatures. Most bacteria are killed by heat at 70 degrees centigrade or above. Fridges and freezers should be set between -22 and five degrees centigrade as most bacteria cannot live at such temperatures. **Be aware of food deteriorating too quickly** as this may mean that the fridge is not cold enough. Always check use-by dates on food as service users with a limited income may economise by buying produce with a limited use-by date.

☺ Activity 30: Infection control (b)

Name three food-poisoning bacteria and where they can be found.

1.

2.

3.

List three ways in which food-poisoning bacteria may be spread.

1.

2.

3.

What precautions should you take when serving food to service users?

What temperature should food be cooked to?

At what temperature should food be stored?

Discuss your answers with your food handling and hygiene trainer or manager.

PERSONAL PROTECTIVE EQUIPMENT

The Personal Protective Equipment at Work Regulations (1992) state that your employer must provide you with protective clothing. You will be provided with a uniform. This should be removed immediately on your arrival home and washed, as it might be contaminated and could spread infection to the outside community or your family.

You will also be provided with plastic aprons to wear when attending to the personal hygiene needs of service users. This will help to protect your uniform from spillages of urine, faeces etc, and prevent cross infection. You must wear a clean apron for every service user you work with, and correctly dispose of it in the clinical waste bag (or double wrapped in plastic bags and placed in an outside bin if a clinical waste bag is not available) when finished.

If you have to work with body fluids and waste or soiled laundry, you will also be provided with gloves. You must wear these, for your own protection and to prevent the spread of infection from one service user to another. You should place any used gloves into a clinical waste bin or double bag and place in an outside waste bin. It is also important that you wash your hands after wearing the gloves.

MEDICATION AND THE OLDER PERSON

According to the *Domiciliary Care: National minimum standards – regulations* (DoH, 2003), the registered manager must ensure that there is a policy on the administration of medicines, and care staff must adhere to procedures for the receipt, recording, storage, handling, administration and disposal of medicines. The policy should include advice on:

- self-medication
- obtaining prescriptions and recording the information
- the recording of medicines
- the handling and storage of medicines
- staff training
- caring for those receiving medication.

SELF-MEDICATION

Where appropriate, service users should be responsible for their own medication. These individuals will usually have a pharmacy-prepared dosset box in which the medication is stored. Suitably trained, designated care staff may have access to this – with the service user's permission. The service user should be assessed by an appropriately trained member of staff in order to establish their suitability to self-medicate.

OBTAINING PRESCRIPTIONS AND RECORDING THE INFORMATION

Care workers need to be familiar with the organisation's policy on arranging repeat prescriptions, collection of dispensed prescriptions and buying over-the-counter remedies. Most domiciliary care agencies will have a policy of not administering or purchasing household medication as many drugs, including household remedies, may interact with other medicines. Requests from a service user to purchase or collect medication should be refused, reported to your line manager and recorded in the care plan. All new medication must be entered on the medication administration record.

THE RECORDING OF MEDICINES

Within the care plan a record is maintained of the medicines that each service user takes, including those who are self-medicating. All medication prompted or administered by the worker should be recorded in the appropriate section of the care plan.

THE HANDLING AND STORAGE OF MEDICINES

It is important that medicines are stored according to the instructions given on the packaging. All medication has a shelf life, which must be checked before it is given. All unused medicines should be returned to a pharmacy for disposal (some pharmacies will collect unused medication). Medicines must not be given to others or should not be disposed of in the sink or toilet.

STAFF TRAINING

The training for care staff must be accredited and must include basic knowledge of how medicines are used and how to recognise and deal with problems in their use. It must also include the principles behind all aspects of the employer's policy on medicines handling and records. The worker should only administer medication if they have had specialist training and it is within their competence.

CARING FOR THOSE RECEIVING MEDICATION

Care staff should monitor the condition of any service user who is receiving medication and should inform the care manager if they are concerned about any change in the service user's condition that may be a result of medication. When a service user dies, medicines should be retained for a period of seven days in case there is a coroner's inquest.

THE ROLE OF THE CARE WORKER IN THE ADMINISTRATION OF MEDICINES

Many of your service users will be taking medication prescribed by their GP. Unless you have received medicines awareness training and you are a designated person, you will not be allowed to administer any medicines to service users. Your responsibility is to support and encourage the service user to take their medication by:

- providing information about the medication that is to be taken
- ensuring that the medication can be swallowed in an appropriate form (for example, tablets or capsules should not be crushed)
- assisting the individual to take their medication (for example, by adjusting their position so they can swallow more easily, or providing a drink)
- making sure that the medication has been taken
- reporting any problems associated with taking the medicine to your care manager.

As a designated person you should only administer prescription drugs from their original packaging, which must be clearly labelled with the dosage and service user's name clearly stated. You should never administer herbal or over the counter remedies eg. aspirin or cough medicine or purchase non-prescription medication on a service user's behalf.

☺ Activity 31: Medication

1. Here are four medicines commonly taken by the service user. Discuss them with your manager.

	Uses	Side effects
Amoxycillin		
Aspirin		
Digoxin		
Insulin		

2. Discuss with your manager your employer's policy on administration of medicines and answer the following questions.

Who is responsible for the ordering of medicines?

Who is responsible for the administration of medicines?

What is the procedure for determining which service user can self-medicate?

What is the procedure for recording medication?

How do you know whether the correct medicine is being given at the correct time, and according to the correct dose?

How are unused medicines disposed of?

SAFETY IN THE COMMUNITY

GENERAL POINTS

- Make sure that you and your employer know your work plan. When working outside of normal office hours always contact the out-of-hours service if there are any delays or emergencies.
- Never carry your house keys and any means of identity together.
- Avoid carrying large amounts of money.
- Vary your route when collecting pensions or money for your service users.
- Avoid quiet deserted areas and, where possible, keep to well-lit roads and bus stops.
- Always park under a streetlight if possible.
- Walk down the centre of the pavement.
- Always walk facing the oncoming traffic for visibility.
- Do not walk with your hands in your pockets, so that you can defend yourself if necessary.
- Always carry a torch with you.
- If you think you are being followed keep walking, cross the road and head to a busy area if possible and ask for help.
- Do not accept lifts unless you know and trust the driver.
- Always carry your mobile phone and some change and a phonecard in case you need to use a payphone.

WHEN ENTERING PREMISES

- If you are in any doubt about your safety, do not enter.
- Be wary if you have to use a lift, especially if there is anyone else inside. Stand by the door so that you can exit if someone you are unsure about enters. Use the stairs if necessary.

WHEN TRAVELLING BY CAR

- Make sure your car is reliable and serviced regularly.
- Ensure you have enough petrol for your journey.
- Have the phone number of your breakdown recovery service to hand.
- Carry change and a phonecard, as well as your mobile phone.
- Do not deviate from your rota. If you do have to, make sure you inform the office.
- Keep valuables out of site and always keep your car doors locked when driving, particularly in stop-start traffic or at traffic lights.
- Never pick up hitchhikers.
- If you think you are being followed, drive to the nearest police station or a busy area where there are other people, such as a petrol station.
- If you experience threatening or aggressive behaviour from another driver always give way.
- Always lock your car door when filling up with petrol.

PARKING YOUR CAR

- Always put valuables in the boot – do not leave them in sight.
- Park in a well-lit place, especially if you think it will be dark when you return to your car.
- Always reverse into a parking space when in a multistorey car park.
- Ensure you have you car keys ready when you return to your car and be aware of people around you and your environment.

ENTERING THE SERVICE USER'S HOME

- Do not enter if you are in any doubt about your safety – call the branch or out-of-hours service.
- If the service user has a visitor who is aggressive or abusive towards you, inform the service user that you are leaving and call the branch or out-of-hours service immediately.
- Be wary of unlit corridors.

SECURITY IN THE SERVICE USER'S HOME

- Before you leave make sure that everything is to hand for your service user (for example, phone, drink, pendant alarm, torch). Turn off any electrical appliances, such as electric blankets, fires, televisions etc, and extinguish lights according to the service user's requirements.
- Make sure that doors and windows are securely closed and locked when you leave the service user's home. **Always double check the door you are leaving by to ensure that it is properly locked.**

KEY HOLDING

Many service users will not be able to open the door for you. In this instance, your employer will have a procedure in place and you must familiarise yourself with this procedure. It may be that you have to collect a key from the office or a neighbour. Or there may be a key safe placed on an outside wall where the key is stored. If this is the case, it is essential that you know the code to access the key. It is extremely important that you follow basic procedures to ensure the safety of the service user if you are holding a key or key code to their home:

- you must not attach anything to the key that identifies where it is for
- you must keep the key safe while it is in your possession, do not leave it unattended at any time
- you must not let anyone know that you have a key to a client's home
- you must not make a copy of the key
- you must inform your manager immediately if you lose the key
- if the client's care package ceases, or is suspended, you must return the key to your manager immediately
- if you have the number of the key safe, you must never record the client's details against that number
- always ensure that the key is returned to the key safe and that the safe is locked before leaving
- ensure that you know your employer's policy on key holding.

☺ Activity 32: Security (a)

Identify the various security measures that your employer has in place. Make a note of these below.

RISKS OF VIOLENCE AND HOW TO MINIMISE DANGERS

Violence at work may include verbal abuse, threatening behaviour and assault. In order to protect yourself, you will need to know which service users may become violent or abusive, the sorts of situations that might lead to violence and abuse and how you might reduce the dangers. Managing violence is covered by the general duties outlined in the Health and Safety at Work Act (1974) and *The Management of Health and Safety at Work Regulations* (1999). In order to protect staff from violence, the Health and Safety Executive (2001) states that your employer should consider the following questions.

- Is there a reporting system in place?
- Do staff know how to report incidents and are they encouraged to do so?
- Is an assessment of risks of violence made and are problems identified?
- Have a range of preventive measures been considered (eg. environment, personal security, training, staffing levels)?
- Are preventive measures implemented?
- Is the effectiveness of these measures monitored?

A confused and disorientated service user might have a tendency to experience mood swings and aggression. This is often the result of stress, frustration and anger, as the confused and disorientated service user cannot understand what is happening in their environment. You can reduce any potential danger by:

- following your workplace's procedures for preventing and dealing with violence
- knowing what might trigger a violent episode
- recognising early signs of potential aggression (eg. fear, anxiety or stress)
- regularly assessing the risk of potential violence
- reporting abusive situations promptly and accurately in the incident book
- regularly attending training in the management of violent and abusive behaviour.

☺ Activity 33: Security (b)

Find out where your employer's policy on managing violence and aggression is kept. Discuss this with your manager. Write short notes under the following headings.

Where is the policy kept?

What is my responsibility in relation to this policy?

How is aggression or violence managed in my workplace?

How might aggression or violence be prevented?

Where is the policy on lone working kept?

What support does the out-of-hours service offer?

💡 Test your knowledge

MAINTAINING HEALTH AND SAFETY AT WORK
The following questions are intended to 'test' your learning. They are not intended to catch you out in any way; rather, they give you an opportunity to review what you have learned, and to revisit and/or revise key parts of this chapter.

1. What are the main responsibilities of the employer under the Health and Safety at Work Act (1974)?

2. What are the bones of the spine called?

3. List the four actions that a moving and handling risk assessment should include?

4. In first aid what does **D R A B** stand for?

5. List three ways in which micro-organisms can be spread.

6. List three precautions you should take when handling food.

7. Where should you dispose of your plastic apron?

8. How are unused medicines disposed of?

9. How would you deal with a minor wound?

10. How would you deal with a minor burn?

Please refer to the answers in **Appendix one** (p117).

You have now completed the third chapter. Please ensure that you and your mentor complete the induction record on the next page, and that you place the answers to the learning activities in your **portfolio**.

When the induction record has been completed, place it in your **portfolio**, together with your **induction plan** and the answers to each of the **learning activities** you have completed.

✍ My induction record

© Malcolm Day 2005

1. Name of domiciliary care worker ....

2. Name of manager/supervisor ....

3. Name of employer ....

4. Induction start date ....

5. Expected date of induction completion ....

6. This is to confirm that .... (name of care worker)
   has satisfactorily completed all of the learning activities related to:

Standard 3.0 Maintain safety at work
     3.1 Health and safety
     3.2 Moving and handling
     3.3 Fire safety
     3.4 Emergency first aid
     3.5 Infection prevention and control
     3.6 Medication and healthcare procedures
     3.7 Security.

7. Any comments from care worker/supervisor or mentor?

Signed (domiciliary care worker): .... Date: ....

Signed (supervisor/mentor): .... Date: ....

Chapter four

Pavilion

Chapter four

Communicating effectively

AIMS OF THIS CHAPTER

This chapter will build on **Chapter one**, which examined your responsibility in relation to the care values, confidentiality and care planning. When you have completed this chapter you will have achieved the following standards:

Standard 4.0 Communicate effectively
      4.1 Encourage communication
      4.2 Use communication techniques
      4.3 The principles of good record keeping.

This unit also relates to the following units of the new Level 2 NVQ in Health and Social Care:

- **HSC21:** Communicate with and complete records for individuals
- **HSC22:** Support the health and safety of yourself and individuals
- **HSC24:** Ensure your own actions support the care, protection and well-being of individuals.

COMMUNICATING EFFECTIVELY

The reasons people communicate are to:

- give information (eg. instructions on taking medication)
- obtain information (eg. a care history)
- meet emotional needs (eg. finding out how people feel)
- exchange ideas (eg. evaluation of care plan)
- meet social needs (eg. participating in quiz or a game of bingo)
- meet physical needs (eg. undertaking a risk assessment).

When we communicate with each other, we are sending and receiving messages. These messages are encoded by a *sender* and decoded by a *receiver*.

$$\text{SENDER} \longrightarrow \text{RECEIVER}$$
$$\text{(Encodes)} \qquad\qquad \text{(Decodes)}$$

Sometimes, we send messages that are intentional and at other times the messages we send are unintentional. Unintentional messages can be conveyed by the tone of our voice or our body language. The messages we send will influence the way others respond to us.

However we send a message, we must try to ensure that those who are receiving or decoding the message are aware that it is genuine and purposeful. However, there may be occasions when a message is misinterpreted, or there may be barriers to the communication process. Some barriers to communication might be:

- environmental: excessive background noise (eg. television)
- language: use of jargon or abbreviations that the service user cannot understand
- perceptual: the service user may have a hearing loss or visual impairment
- illness: the service user may be confused, disorientated or depressed.

ENCOURAGING COMMUNICATION
Most people assume that in order to communicate, people have to talk to each other. However, this is not necessarily the case, as much of our communication is non-verbal. In other words, we communicate through:

- facial expression – can give an indication of your underlying feelings

- eye contact – appropriate eye contact can show that you are interested in a conversation

- posture – your posture should show that you are alert and paying attention

- gesture – nodding your head shows that you are interested

- touch – a handshake is a sign of friendship and can signal the start or the end of conversation

- proximity – close personal contact (a hug, for example) can sometimes be reassuring

- tone of voice – can indicate concern for an individual.

Care workers are encouraged to use **active listening** techniques in order to encourage communication and maximise the communication process. Active listeners focus on:

- what is being said verbally (ie. content)
- how the person is saying it (ie. tone of voice)
- what is being communicated non-verbally (ie. body language).

USING NON-VERBAL COMMUNICATION TECHNIQUES
Non-verbal behaviour can often be used to initiate or sustain a conversation. This is particularly important when meeting a service user and their family for the first time, as they are likely to be anxious, or even distressed. In order to encourage and sustain a dialogue, it is important that you pay attention and show concern. You can do this by:

- **S – sitting** squarely and opposite the individual

- **O –** having an **open** posture, arms unfolded with no physical barriers between you

- **L – leaning** forward, slightly towards the individual, but not too close

- **E –** maintain **eye** contact, a steady gaze, but don't stare

- **R – relax** and show that you are listening.

SOLER

These tips come from a book called *The Skilled Helper* (Egan, 1975).

USING VERBAL COMMUNICATION TECHNIQUES

Only about 10% of our communication is actually spoken. It is very important that you make the most of your conversations with service users and their families, as this will enable you to establish relationships and accurately identify their needs and feelings. Much of this information can be collected through careful questioning, and it is important that you consider the different techniques that might be used to accurately and effectively collect information without creating too much distress. For example, you might use:

- closed questions
- open questions
- process questions
- clarification.

CLOSED QUESTIONS

For example: 'Would you like an extra pillow, Mr Smith?' The breathless person need only reply 'Yes' or 'No'. A more complex question would need a longer answer and cause further breathlessness and discomfort.

OPEN QUESTIONS

For example: 'Tell me about your family, Mr Smith.' This will enable you to start up a conversation.

PROCESS QUESTIONS

For example: 'What did you think the doctor was saying, Mr Smith?' This type of questioning can give you an indication as to how the individual understands their situation.

CLARIFICATION

For example: 'I think you said that this made you feel worse. Is that right, Mr Smith?' This is a useful way of checking or summarising the outcomes of a conversation.

☺ Activity 34: Developing your communication techniques

Think back to a conversation you recently had with a service user. Using the guidelines on page 81, think about how you might have improved your questioning technique. Take one specific question that you have recently asked. How might you improve it?

Record your answers below.

How I might have improved my questioning technique

How I have improved my question

COMMUNICATING WITH THE SENSORY IMPAIRED

Some older people may have difficulty communicating because of poor eyesight or hearing. You can assist service users who have visual impairment by making sure that their eyesight is tested regularly, that their spectacles are clean and worn properly, and that their possessions are kept in the same, familiar place. You could also learn the correct way to guide and assist a partially sighted person while they are walking, and find out what visual aids are available in your nursing home, such as large print books and newspapers or talking books.

You can support service users with hearing impairment by making sure that their hearing aid is tested regularly, that it is clean and worn properly and that the battery is not flat. You can also learn the correct way to replace a hearing aid battery, or talk to colleagues about how people with hearing impairments use sign language. You can find out what aids are available, such as flashing lights instead of telephone ringtones or doorbells.

COMMUNICATING WITH THOSE WHO HAVE MEMORY LOSS

Failure of memory is one of the many barriers that may prevent effective communication between yourself and the service user. Therefore, it is very important to try and keep the channels of communication open at all times, to avoid frustration, anxiety and potentially aggressive outbursts. It is important to find out the preferred name of the service user and to develop a good working relationship. You should attempt to reduce background distractions, such as excessive noise, so that the service user's concentration can be improved. You should also ensure that the service user is making the best use of their hearing aid, spectacles or other sensory aids that are provided. In addition, you should:

- speak clearly, slowly and distinctly
- use simple words and short sentences
- ask one question at a time and wait for a reply
- use the same words when repeating statements
- encourage the service user to talk and express their personal views without causing distress to others
- avoid correcting any mistakes or arguing with the service user
- avoid using the word 'why' as this might be perceived by the service user as being confrontational
- initiate contact by holding the service user's hand and looking at them in the face
- maintain eye contact and communication through occasional hugs or cuddles
- keep an eye on the service user's tone of voice, facial expressions and posture, in order to assess whether they are being understood.

These tips come from the book *A Pathway to NVQs in Care: An underpinning knowledge* (Ironbar, 2002).

COMMUNICATING WITH THOSE WHO ARE CONFUSED

A service user may be confused, and experience a limited concentration span and disorientation during which they are unaware of their surroundings. In such cases, the service user often has difficulty in finding the right words to name people or objects that they recognise. They might often become agitated or restless, and may act aggressively towards others. It is important:

- to call the service user by their preferred name

- to establish trust and a good working relationship with the service user

- to maintain their dignity and independence by praising or rewarding appropriate behaviour

- that the care worker continues to orientate the service user to everyday information using a variety of approaches (such as cue cards, colourful pictures or personal artefacts like family pictures)

- that any misunderstandings the service user may have are dealt with tactfully in order to avoid arguments.

A confused service user may accuse someone of stealing their belongings. This could be a way of preserving their self-esteem, in order to maintain some control in their life. You should:

- assess the environment for any forms of excessive stimulation (such as a loud television or radio, or whispering nearby) that may lead to misinterpretation

- avoid using the word 'why' as this might be perceived as being confrontational by the service user

- try and divert the service user's attention by engaging them in some recreational activities

- reassure the service user regarding any underlying fear or anxiety

- explain to others in the vicinity that the service user's behaviour is the result of illness and not a deliberate act of malice.

These tips come from the book *A Pathway to NVQs in Care: An underpinning knowledge* (Ironbar, 2002).

COMMUNICATING WITH THE BEREAVED

People who are dying, or who have been bereaved, often go through a series of stages as they adjust to their situation, or adjust to the loss of a friend or loved one. As a care worker, you are responsible for providing support to these individuals. Therefore, it is important that you recognise how each stage of the grieving process might affect your relationship with a service user who is dying or bereaved. The stages of adjustment associated with the grieving process include:

- denial
- anger
- withdrawal or depression
- acceptance.

DENIAL
The person who is dying refuses to believe that he or she is going to die. The bereaved person can't believe that they have lost a loved one.

ANGER
The dying or bereaved person is angry about their situation.

WITHDRAWAL OR DEPRESSION
The dying or bereaved person is sad, full of despondency and uncommunicative.

ACCEPTANCE
The dying person accepts that death is near and becomes peaceful. The bereaved person's life begins to return to normality.

Of course, not everyone will regularly and consistently display behaviour associated with every one of these stages. Some individuals may demonstrate an extreme grief reaction and exhibit all of these behaviours at once. Others may find it difficult to move on and become 'fixated' at a particular stage. For example, a severe and prolonged depression for several years is not uncommon among people who have been bereaved.

It is important that you listen carefully to the wishes of the dying person, particularly with regard to how he or she wants to die, and who should be with them at the time of their death. Sometimes these wishes might appear inappropriate, or they might be contrary to the wishes of a relative or loved one. If so, it is important that you seek help and advice from your supervisor.

If you are supporting a bereaved family member or friend, it is important that you listen to their wishes carefully, and provide them with adequate time and privacy to grieve. You will also need to check that they have been given the correct information about what will happen after someone dies, and the support services that are available to them.

AND DON'T FORGET...
Caring for a dying person or supporting bereaved relatives can be very stressful, so don't dismiss or suppress your own feelings or reactions to a bereavement. You will find it helpful to discuss these with a friend or an experienced colleague at work. It is likely that they will have been through a similar situation, and they will not think any the less of you for describing how upset you feel.

PRINCIPLES OF GOOD RECORD KEEPING

Care plans, needs assessments, case reviews and day files are required as legal records of care. Keeping certain confidential notes and records relating to individual service users is also an essential part of the communication and day-to-day running of domiciliary care services.

According to the *Domiciliary Care: National minimum standards – regulations* (DoH, 2003), care records kept in the home should be:

- legible, factual, signed and dated.
- relevant and useful.

Care records should be factual, consistent and accurate. They should be:

- written as soon as possible after an event has occurred, providing current information on the care and condition of the service user

- written clearly, legibly and in such a manner that they cannot be erased

- written in such a manner that any alterations or additions are dated, timed and signed in such a way that the original entry can still be clearly read

- accurately dated, timed and signed or otherwise identified, with the name of the author being printed alongside the first entry

- readable on any photocopies (ie. care records should be written in black ink)

- written, wherever applicable, with the involvement of the service user

- clear, unambiguous (preferably concise) and written in terms that the service user can understand

- written so as to comply with the Race Relations Act (1976)

- written so as to comply with the Disability Discrimination Act (1995).

Care records should be relevant and useful. They should:

- identify problems that have arisen and the action taken to rectify them

- provide evidence of the care planned, the decisions made, the care delivered and the information shared

- provide evidence of actions agreed with the service user (including consent to care and/or consent to disclose information).

In addition, care records should not include:

- unnecessary abbreviations or jargon
- meaningless phrases, irrelevant speculation or offensive subjective statements
- irrelevant personal opinions regarding the service user.

The rules governing the recording and use of service user information have been laid down by *The Caldicott Report* (DoH, 1995). The key requirements of this report are that you must:

- justify a purpose for recording and using service user information
- only record and use information when it is absolutely necessary
- use only the minimum information required
- only access information on a strict 'need to know' basis
- be aware of your responsibilities concerning the recording and use of service user information
- understand and comply with the law (eg. the Data Protection Act (1998)).

The *Domiciliary Care: National minimum standards – regulations* (DoH, 2003) state that care workers should be fostering an atmosphere of openness and respect, in which the service users, family, friends and representatives all feel valued and that their opinions and rights matter. In the case of record keeping, this can be done by encouraging care workers to involve the service user whenever records are being written. If this is done, not only can the service user be more actively involved in their own care, but the need for the recording can be explained and understood. By developing an atmosphere of 'working together' with the service user, anxieties will be greatly reduced.

Standard 16 of the *Domiciliary Care: National minimum standards – regulations* (DoH, 2003) relates to the degree to which service users' rights and best interests are safeguarded by a service provider's record-keeping policies and procedures. Specific standards include the following.

- All records are secure, up to date and in good order and are constructed, maintained and used in accordance with the Data Protection Act (1998) and other statutory requirements and are kept for the requisite amount of time.

- Service users or their representatives have access to their records and information held about them by the service provider and are facilitated in obtaining access when necessary.

- Individual records and service provider records are secure, up to date and in good order; and are constructed, maintained and used in accordance with the Data Protection Act (1998) and other statutory requirements.

THE DATA PROTECTION ACT (1998)

The Data Protection Act (1998) sets standards governing the storage and processing of personal data held in manual records and on computers. The Act works in two ways: it gives individuals (data subjects) certain rights, while requiring those who record and use personal information (data controllers) to be open about their use of that information and to follow sound and proper practices (the data protection principles). Organisations that hold manual or computerised service user or employee records are covered by the Act. According to the Act, there are eight main principles under which personal data should be kept and collected. Personal data should:

- be obtained fairly and lawfully
- be held for specified and lawful purposes
- be processed in accordance with the person's rights under the Act
- be adequate, relevant and not excessive in relation to that purpose
- be kept accurate and up to date
- not be kept for longer than is necessary for its given purpose
- be subject to appropriate safeguards against unauthorised use, loss or damage.

One of the most important aspects of the Act is that personal data may be processed only if the service user has given their consent. All files kept about residents or staff should be confidential and, according to the Act, service users should know what records are being kept about them and why they are being kept.

Service users should also be given access to what is said about them in any personal records maintained by the care worker in the service user's home. Information should be withheld only in exceptional circumstances. All information, particularly sensitive or confidential information, must be stored as securely as possible within the service user's home. Manual records, such as daily log books, should be returned to the service provider when the log is fully completed and replaced with a new one. When returned to the service provider, the log book (and the service user plan if the care has concluded) should be kept in locked filing cabinets. This should preferably be in an office that is locked when unattended. When working on confidential files at the service provider's office, care must be taken that they are put away securely and not left out on a desk where people could walk by and see them. Where data is stored electronically on a computer, the following steps should be considered:

- check regularly on the accuracy of data being entered (remember that a home may be liable for inaccurate or erroneous data)

- ensure that the computer system is secure by checking that it has a backup system, any lost data can be recovered and that backups are stored in a safe and secure place

- ensure that all staff who need to use the computer system are thoroughly trained in its use

- ensure that passwords are being used for access to different parts of the system, that these are regularly changed and not abused by being passed on to people who should not have them

- use screen blanking to ensure that personal data is not left on screen when not in use by authorised staff

- review the terminal positions to ensure that unauthorised staff or service users cannot casually view personal data on screens

- ensure that confidential or private printouts are stored securely and safely, and that they are collected immediately if printed onto a networked printer.

With regard to the use of service user records kept within the service user's home, the *Domiciliary Care: National minimum standards – regulations* (DoH, 2003) state that the care worker should ensure that the following requirements are met:

- records should be legible, factual, signed and dated, and kept in a safe place in the home, as agreed with the service user, their relatives or representative

- records should be tracked if transferred, with a note made in the new daily log book

- daily log books should be returned to the service provider's office once full, and replaced if care is ongoing

- care plans should also be returned to the service provider on conclusion of the care

- records should be stored securely in the office and arranged so that the record can easily be found if needed urgently

- records should be stored closed when not in use, so that contents are not seen accidentally

- records should be inaccessible to members of the public and not left where they might be looked at by unauthorised persons, even for short periods

- records should be held in secure storage with clear labelling indicating sensitivity (though not indicating the reason for sensitivity), permitted access, and the availability of secure means of destruction (eg. shredding) or secure confidential storage.

With regard to electronic records, care staff must:

- always log-out of any computer system or application when work on it is finished

- not leave a terminal unattended and logged-in

- not share log-ins with other people

- not reveal passwords to others

- change passwords at regular intervals to prevent anyone else using them

- avoid using short passwords, or using names or words that are known to be associated with them (eg. children's or pets' names or birthdays)

- always clear the screen of a previous patient's information before seeing another

- use a password-protected screen-saver to prevent casual viewing of patient information by others.

Finally, please remember…

- Accurate and timely record keeping is essential to good care practice.

- Care records (eg. observation charts, records of daily activities, risk assessment charts and care plans) are all legal documents. You must complete them in a clear, accurate and objective way.

- You must be familiar with, and always follow, your employer's policies and procedures on what, where, when and how to complete individual care records.

- Observing the rules concerning the appropriate storage, security and disclosure of care records will ensure that service user information remains confidential.

☺ Activity 35: Principles of record keeping

Please complete the following statements.

1. *The Caldicott Report* (DoH, 1995) says care workers must ensure that service user information is

2. The *Domiciliary Care: National minimum standards – regulations* (DoH, 2003) for manual record keeping say that care workers must

3. When recording information in the service user's care records, I must

Discuss your answers with your mentor.

💡 Test your knowledge

COMMUNICATING EFFECTIVELY

The following questions are intended to 'test' your learning. They are not intended to catch you out in any way; rather, they give you an opportunity to review what you have learned, and to revisit and/or revise key parts of this chapter.

1. Give three reasons for communicating with other people.

2. How often do we communicate through the spoken word?

3. What is **S O L E R** ?

4. Give three ways in which people are able to communicate.

5. State three different types of questions.

6. What are the stages of grieving?

7. What is the Data Protection Act?

8. Give three key requirements of *The Caldicott Report*.

9. Give three precautions to be taken when using care records in the service user's home.

10. List three precautions to be taken when using electronic records.

Please refer to the answers in **Appendix one** (p118).

You have now completed the fourth chapter. Please ensure that you and your mentor complete the induction record on the next page, and that you place the answers to the learning activities in your **portfolio**.

When the induction record has been completed, place it in your **portfolio**, together with your **induction plan** and the answers to each of the **learning activities** you have completed.

✍ My induction record

© Malcolm Day 2005

1. Name of domiciliary care worker ....

2. Name of manager/supervisor ....

3. Name of employer ....

4. Induction start date ....

5. Expected date of induction completion ....

6. This is to confirm that .... (name of care worker)
   has satisfactorily completed all of the learning activities related to:

Standard 4.0 Communicate effectively
    4.1 Encourage communication
    4.2 Use communication techniques
    4.3 The principles of good record keeping.

7. Any comments from care worker/supervisor or mentor?

Signed (domiciliary care worker): .... Date: ....

Signed (supervisor/mentor): .... Date: ....

Chapter five

Recognise and respond to abuse and neglect

Pavilion

Chapter five

Recognise and respond to abuse and neglect

AIMS OF THIS CHAPTER

This chapter will build on **Chapter one**, which examined your responsibility in relation to care values, confidentiality and care planning. When you have completed this chapter, you will have achieved the following standards:

Standard 5.0 Recognise and respond to abuse and neglect

5.1 Legislation, policies and procedures

5.2 Understand the nature of abuse and neglect

5.3 Recognise the signs and symptoms of abuse and neglect

5.4 Understand how to respond to suspected abuse or neglect

5.5 Whistle-blowing.

This unit also relates to the following unit of the Level 2 NVQ in Health and Social Care:

■ **HSC24:** Ensure your own actions support the care, protection and well-being of individuals.

LEGISLATION, POLICIES AND PROCEDURES

Vulnerable people are protected against abuse in the same way as any other person, through both the criminal and civil courts. If a person commits theft, assault or any other criminal act against a vulnerable person then they are dealt with through a court of law. In addition, there are also a number of pieces of legislation and guidance that provide a framework relating to the specific prevention of abuse or exploitation of vulnerable adults. For example, *No Secrets* (DoH, 2000) is guidance issued under section seven of the Local Authority Social Services Act (1970), the key measures of which include:

■ granting social services lead status for protecting vulnerable adults

■ granting social services a co-ordinating role in developing local policies and procedures for protecting vulnerable adults

■ a requirement for all relevant agencies to work collaboratively and develop inter-agency policies and procedures.

The Care Standards Act (2000) includes provision for a Protection of Vulnerable Adults (POVA) register to be kept of all those people considered unsuitable to work with vulnerable adults. Care organisations can contribute to this register by reporting any proven cases of abuse, and by referring to the register whenever recruiting new staff (see **Appendix two**).

The Sexual Offences Act (2003) was passed with the aim of protecting vulnerable adults and children from sexual abuse and exploitation. The provisions of the act include:

- the introduction of a number of new offences to protect 'at risk' groups, such as people with learning disabilities and other groups with reduced capacity, such as people with advanced dementia

- strengthening the Sex Offenders Register to ensure that the location of people who have committed serious sex-related crimes are known to the police

- strengthening and clarifying the meaning of 'non-consensual' sex.

The Act introduces a test of 'reasonableness' on consent and a list of circumstances in which it can be presumed that consent was very unlikely to have been given, for example, when the victim was asleep.

The Mental Capacity Act (2005) provides a statutory framework to empower and protect vulnerable people who are not able to make their own decisions. It makes it clear who can take decisions, in which situations, and how they should go about this. It enables people to plan ahead for a time when they may lose capacity. Guidance on the Act is provided in a *Code of Practice* (Department for Constitutional Affairs, 2007) for health and social care workers (see **Appendix three**).

UNDERSTANDING THE NATURE OF ABUSE AND NEGLECT

Each of the service users that you care for has their own life history and unique set of social circumstances. They also have their own preferred ways of doing things. Many of the service users that you care for will have had to make significant adjustments to their lifestyle. They may have been physically disabled by a stroke, or may have had their mobility impaired by continuing ill health. Their ability to maintain an independent lifestyle is likely therefore to be severely restricted. As a result, the service user is likely to be dependent on you to meet their basic human needs for food and drink, to maintain personal hygiene, to eliminate, etc. Many service users will be anxious and frightened that their individual needs won't be met. Others may become angry or frustrated as they believe their identity, individuality and independence have been lost. As a care worker, it is important that you:

- explain in simple and straightforward language why you are providing care
- explain what your role is and how this is bound by confidentiality
- encourage service users to ask questions and tell you how they feel
- encourage them to tell you their likes and dislikes.

You will also need to know when to ask for help if the service user is showing signs of difficulty in adjusting. Remember, the service user may be exhibiting signs that are very similar to loss or bereavement (**Chapter three**) – you should report any concerns you may have to your supervisor.

Older people who are dependent on others for their care needs are in a potentially vulnerable position, and may be at risk from those who might abuse the power and influence they have as a carer. It is the legal and moral responsibility of everyone working in the community to respect the rights of service users and to protect them from physical or mental harm at all times. Failure to do so may constitute abuse.

Perpetrators of abuse can be any people who are in a position of trust with a service user, and may include partners, children or other relatives, carers, friends or neighbours, volunteer care workers, professional healthcare staff or care workers themselves. Care workers should notice when service users are at risk from, or experiencing, neglect or abuse, and should respond appropriately to ensure that individual service users are protected. The factors that are known to contribute to abuse and exploitation include:

- prolonged stress among the caregivers or care workers
- feelings of resentment and hostility towards the service user
- deeply held prejudices and stereotypes towards particular social groups (eg. the elderly)
- financial dependency on the service user by a child or spouse
- unrestricted access to the service user's finances by child or spouse
- poor levels of practical competence in caring for the older person
- inadequate monitoring or supervision of a carer or care worker.

TYPES OF ABUSE AND NEGLECT
Described in local *No Secrets* (DoH, 2000) policies, the definition of abuse is that it is:

'a single or a repeated act, omission or lack of appropriate action, occurring within a relationship of care or trust, which causes distress, harm or injury'.

This definition allows several different types of abuse to be recognised, including neglect, physical abuse, psychological abuse, sexual abuse, racial or cultural abuse and financial abuse. These are defined by *Domiciliary Care: National minimum standards – regulations* (DoH, 2003) as follows.

Physical abuse can take many forms, including hitting, slapping, burning, pushing or restraining. Rough or careless handling may also constitute physical harm, as can giving too much medication or the wrong type of medication.

Neglect occurs where a service user is not provided with adequate care or attention and suffers harm or distress as a result (eg. where a service user is deprived of food, water, heat, clothing, comfort or essential medication).

Psychological abuse means cruelty or verbal insults, including shouting, swearing, frightening, blaming, ignoring, bullying or humiliating a person, even the spreading of rumours or malicious gossip. All service users should be able to live their lives with privacy, dignity, independence and choice (remember **P R I C I D**?) and all information about them should remain confidential. The disclosure of confidential information, for example, by spreading stories or rumours about individuals, could be regarded as psychological or emotional abuse.

Sexual abuse occurs wherever a service user is forced to take part in any sexual activity without their prior consent. Sexual abuse can also take more subtle forms, and any sexual relationship between staff and service users can be considered to be abusive, even if the service user gives their consent. Sexual abuse may also occur when staff are giving personal care to a service user.

Financial abuse is the obtaining of money, valuable possessions, or property through cheating or deception.

Racial or cultural abuse often takes the form of discrimination, prejudice or insults.

In some service users' homes there may be an underlying culture that is indicative of abuse. Staff in these care homes often show a lack of concern or even contempt for service users. There may be a lack of flexibility or choice, a lack of privacy, a lack of respect, unjustified use of restraints or staff entering service users' rooms without due cause. There may also be restrictive practices full of petty rules and restrictions.

THE SIGNS OF ABUSE AND NEGLECT

The following are possible signs that abuse might be occurring. However, it should be remembered that this is not a comprehensive list and other signs and symptoms might be present. Also, the presence of one or more of these signs does not mean that there is absolute proof of abuse; rather, it indicates that abuse might be occurring.

PHYSICAL ABUSE
- Unexplained bruises or cuts, especially where they reflect the shape of an object used, of a hand or of finger marks.
- Loss of hair in clumps or abrasions on the scalp from hair-pulling.
- Unexplained fractures.
- Unexplained burns or scalding.
- Delays in reporting injuries.
- Vague, implausible or inappropriate explanations.
- Multiple injuries or a history of past injuries – especially falls.

NEGLECT
- Debilitation or weakness through malnutrition or dehydration.
- Unexplained weight loss.
- Poor hygiene – unkempt, dirty appearance, clothes or surroundings.
- Inappropriate dress.
- Pressure sores.
- Poor skin condition and poor resistance to infection and disease.

EMOTIONAL ABUSE
- Fearfulness.
- Mood changes, including depression, irritability and unhappiness.

- Low self-esteem.
- Changes in sleep and appetite patterns.
- Withdrawn, self-isolating behaviour.

FINANCIAL ABUSE
- Unexplained loss of money or inability to pay bills.
- Sudden withdrawal of large amounts of money.
- Sudden disappearance of favourite or valuable possessions.
- Loss of pension or building society books, etc.

SEXUAL ABUSE
- Unexplained difficulty in walking.
- Bleeding or bruised genitals.
- Reluctance to be alone with a particular person.
- Sudden changes in behaviour.

RESPONDING TO ABUSE AND NEGLECT

Domiciliary Care: National minimum standards – regulations (DoH, 2003) suggests that care homes should adopt a four-stage approach to the problem of abuse.

1. **Prevention:** as far as is practical or possible, service providers need to aim at preventing abuse from happening at all.

2. **Identification:** where abuse does occur, service providers need to identify it quickly and ensure that it is reported.

3. **Action:** once abuse has been identified, service providers need to take swift action to deal with incidents and ensure the safety of their residents and service users.

4. **Planning:** service providers need to use learning from incidents of abuse in their planning for the future.

The recommendations of the *Domiciliary Care: National minimum standards – regulations* (DoH, 2003) are now explained in more detail.

PREVENTION

The best way of dealing with abuse is to prevent it from happening. Service providers should have policies and procedures in place and should create a culture of awareness among care workers, including an understanding that abuse will not be tolerated. The best way of ensuring that such a culture exists is through effective training and supervision (see **Chapter two**). In addition, it is the responsibility of the service provider to lead by example and, in this respect, all dealings by management should be seen by care workers as fair, transparent and equitable. Care workers should be in no doubt that breaches of policies and procedures against abuse will be identified and, where proved, dealt with immediately and effectively.

IDENTIFICATION

Should it occur, it is vital that any abuse and exploitation is identified and reported. Care workers should be trained to be aware of all forms of potential abuse and exploitation, and should know exactly what to do and who to go to if they have any suspicions or concerns. This will include a need to support whistle-blowing. Very often, staff can feel intimidated by abusers, especially if the abuser is a member of senior staff. There is also often a pressure to stick together with colleagues and many are tempted to keep quiet and ignore the abusive activity. It is especially important that care workers should be in no doubt that they will be supported if they take the step of reporting abuse and that to keep quiet about an abusive situation may in itself constitute a disciplinary or even criminal act.

ACTION

Any report or suggestion of abuse, no matter how minor, should be taken seriously, immediately investigated and appropriate action should be taken. These investigations should be fair and transparent and, if care workers are involved, conducted within the context of employment law. The consent or co-operation of the victim to an investigation is a key element in any action taken and trust is often a key element in obtaining that consent. The victims of abuse often feel intimidated to keep silent or fear the repercussions of speaking out. They may also feel confused or unworthy and do not know whom to trust.

PLANNING

It is vital that care organisations learn from occurrences of abuse and that this informs the way that they operate in the future, for example, through staff training or the use of advocacy services.

ABUSE PROCEDURES

The immediate safety or health of the victim is the first concern. Care workers should talk to the victim and assess the situation, summoning help, giving first aid and calling for medical support, an ambulance or the police as necessary. If the abuser is still present, staff should attempt to calm the situation, but should not place themselves at risk.

If the situation is not an emergency, all suspicions and events should be reported to the person in charge. The person in charge should then investigate the suspicion by collecting evidence and by talking to the service user. Tact and sensitivity are important in this process and it may sometimes be necessary for a care worker known to the service user to talk to them rather than the person in charge.

In situations where the service user says they will tell the care worker but asks the care worker not to tell anyone else, the service user should be advised that they cannot keep that confidentiality and must, by policy, inform the manager or person in charge. However, they should reassure the victim that their information will be treated as confidential and that the service provider will not necessarily proceed with an investigation without their consent – unless there has been a criminal act and the law has been broken, or unless the alleged abuse involves others at risk.

Consent is vital. In general, the victims of abuse do not have to take action against their abuser, and have the right not to. This is particularly common where the abuser may be a son or a daughter or another member of the family. If the suspected victim does not want the incident to be taken further, their wishes must be respected unless the victim is:

■ in physical danger
■ incapable of making an informed decision themselves
■ not the only person at risk.

The underlying rule is that a person has the right to decide how they want to be helped – or if they want to be helped at all. Where a service user is considered incapable of making an informed decision or of giving consent, the person in charge should discuss the situation with close relatives or guardians. Possible risks and outcomes need to be carefully explained to the victim so that an informed decision can be made.

All cases of abuse where the victim gives consent should be referred to social services without delay. In situations where there is evidence of a criminal act, the case should be reported immediately to the police by the manager or person in charge. This is particularly important in cases of suspected sexual abuse, where the police will want to gather forensic evidence (eg. DNA) as rapidly as possible. Referral to the police or social services should include the following information:

■ personal details of the victim
■ the referrer's details
■ the substance of the allegation
■ details of the alleged abuser
■ details of incidents or events, including dates, places, injuries, witnesses
■ whether or not consent has been given to take the matter further.

Once a referral has been made, social services will then work to its own guidelines and procedures, and care workers should ensure that they co-operate. All facts, incidents, assessments and discussions related to the suspicions should be recorded clearly and accurately in the service user's care plan as soon after the incident as possible. Opinion should be avoided and only facts should be reported. Such records are strictly confidential and should be kept securely and safely, according to the Data Protection Act (1998). They may be used as evidence in a future criminal investigation (see **Principles of good record keeping** in **Chapter four**).

Where, in line with the victim's wishes, no referral to social services is made, alternative courses of action should be considered and the service user given appropriate support. In the case of a care worker being the alleged abuser, the service provider should proceed with disciplinary action and an internal investigation in line with the service provider's disciplinary policy. The action of the care worker may constitute grounds for dismissal through gross misconduct, even if no criminal case is pursued. Here it should be remembered that the burden of proof in civil law is not as stringent as that in criminal law. Careful notes should be kept, outlining the exact suspicions and the action taken. In the case of a relative or carer being the alleged abuser, the home may arrange with the service user to restrict visits or to have only accompanied visits. In all cases, the situation should be carefully monitored.

Local social services departments will always be willing to advise individual service providers who have suspicions of abuse and there are several organisations that run confidential helplines and offer similar advice. Service providers must also be prepared to accept that, in some cases of abuse, little action can be taken beyond continued support, recording and monitoring, because of limitations in the law and the victim not wanting to proceed. However, in all cases, detailed written records should be kept in a secure place and all staff should work together to minimise the risk of further abuse.

Once a referral has been made to social services, a care assessor or social care worker will investigate and an assessment will be made of the needs of the victim and the victim's carers. A case conference may well then be arranged and a package of care and support set in place as appropriate. Social services will work hand in hand with the police throughout this process and may continue to monitor the situation for some time.

The police, for their part, have a duty to investigate any possible criminal offences, and this will include interviewing victims, witnesses and suspects and gathering evidence. This process may not always end in criminal proceedings, but early involvement will give the police the best opportunity to conduct their investigations effectively. Cases of suspected sexual abuse should always be reported to the police immediately.

NATIONAL MINIMUM STANDARDS FOR THE PREVENTION OF ABUSE AND NEGLECT

Domiciliary Care: National minimum standards – regulations (DoH, 2003) states that service users' privacy and dignity must be respected and upheld at all times, and in particular that:

- personal care and support is provided in a way that maintains and respects privacy, dignity and the lifestyle of the person receiving care at all times

- all care workers use the term of address preferred by the service user

- all care workers are instructed during their induction on how to treat service users with respect

- service users should be enabled to exercise their legal rights

- service users must be safeguarded from physical, financial, material, psychological, sexual or discriminatory abuse, or abuse through neglect, self-harm or degrading treatment, deliberate intent, negligence or ignorance

- care workers are responsive to the race, culture, religion, age, disability, gender and sexuality of the person receiving care and their relatives and representatives.

Domiciliary Care: National minimum standards – regulations (DoH, 2003) also states that:

- procedures should be in place for responding to suspicion or evidence of abuse or neglect (including whistle-blowing) in accordance with the Public Interest Disclosure Act (1998) and Department of Health guidance, *No Secrets* (2000)

- all allegations and incidents of abuse should be followed up promptly and the action taken should be recorded

- care workers who may be unsuitable to work with vulnerable adults should be referred, in accordance with the Care Standards Act (2000), for consideration for inclusion on the Protection of Vulnerable Adults (POVA) register

- physical or verbal aggression by service users must be understood and dealt with appropriately by staff, and physical intervention or restraint used only as a last resort

- service users should have access to their personal financial records, be able to safely store their money and valuables, be free to consult on their finances in private and be free to gain advice on personal insurance

- care workers should not be involved in assisting the making of, or benefiting from, service users' wills.

Where service users control their own money, then *Domiciliary Care: National minimum standards – regulations* (DoH, 2003) states that:

- safeguards to protect the interests of the service user must be in place

- written records of all transactions are maintained

- no care worker should benefit in *any* way from a service user, their family or their executor at any time

- no care worker can be involved in any legal matter relating to a service user, their family or their executor at any time

- the service provider must ensure that there is a policy and procedure for the investigation of allegations of financial irregularities and the involvement of the police, social services and professional bodies

- where service users are unable to take responsibility for the management of their own finances, this should be recorded on the risk assessment, and action taken to minimise the risk.

WHISTLE-BLOWING

Code of Practice for Employers of Social Care Workers (GSCC, 2002b) states that employers must:

> *'Establish and promote procedures for social care workers to report dangerous, discriminatory, abusive or exploitative behaviour and practice.'*

Further, the *Code of Practice for Social Care Workers* (GSCC, 2002a) states that social care workers must inform their:

> *'employer or an appropriate authority where the practice of colleagues may be unsafe or adversely affecting standards of care.'*

This reporting of unsafe or discriminatory practice is known as 'whistle-blowing'.

The relationship between carer and service user is based on mutual trust. This is recognised by the *Code of Practice for Social Care Workers* (GSCC, 2002a), which states that social care workers must:

> *'(2) strive to establish and maintain the trust and confidence of service users and carers. This includes:*
>
> *2.1 Being honest and trustworthy;*
>
> *2.2 Communicating in an appropriate, open, accurate and straightforward way;*
>
> *2.3 Respecting confidential information and clearly explaining agency policies about confidentiality to service users and carers;*
>
> *2.4. Being reliable and dependable;*
>
> *2.5 Honouring work commitments, agreements and arrangements and, when it is not possible to do so, explaining why to service users and carers;*
>
> *2.6 Declaring issues that might create conflicts of interest and making sure that they do not influence your judgement or practice; and*
>
> *2.7 Adhering to policies and procedures about accepting gifts and money from service users and carers.'*

It is important that service users are allowed to make choices and to take control of their lives as much as possible. Working in a collaborative way enables the service user to maintain some degree of independence. This is called 'empowerment'. This method of working is recognised by the *Code of Practice for Social Care Workers* (GSCC, 2002a), which states that social care workers must:

'(1) protect the rights of service users and carers. This includes:

1.1 Treating each person as an individual;

1.2 Respecting and, where appropriate, promoting the individual views and wishes of both service users and carers;

1.3 Supporting service users' rights to control their lives and make informed choices about the services they receive;

1.4 Respecting and maintaining the dignity and privacy of service users;

1.5 Promoting equal opportunities for service users and carers; and

1.6 Respecting diversity and different cultures and values.'

The individual rights of service users are also recognised by the GSCC codes of practice and by the Commission for Social Care Inspection (CSCI). For example, in their publication *Care Homes for Older People: National minimum standards* (2005), CSCI indicate that service users have the right to:

- privacy and dignity
- choice and control
- express their cultural and spiritual needs
- health and well-being
- socialise and participate in social activities
- good food
- a clean, comfortable and safe home
- protection from harm and abuse.

The rights of individual service users are protected by legislation. For example, the Human Rights Act (1998) includes an individual's right to:

- freedom from torture and inhuman or degrading treatment
- liberty and security of person
- respect for private and family life, home and correspondence
- freedom of thought, conscience and religion
- freedom of expression
- freedom of assembly and association
- peaceful enjoyment of possessions and protection of property.

It is important that carers support service user rights by:

- making sure that *care workers* understand your organisation's policies and guidelines relating to the rights of individuals
- ensuring that *service users* are made fully aware of your organisation's complaints procedures
- discussing choices and preferences with service users

- ensuring that professional colleagues are made aware of service user's choices and preferences
- supporting service users to maintain their rights and independence
- refusing to participate in discriminatory or prejudicial behaviour.

Treating people less favourably than others in the same position because of their ability, age, gender, race, sexuality, is known as discrimination. This is potentially destructive to the individual and may lead to loss of self-esteem. The different types of discrimination might include:

- ignoring the needs of individuals who are different
- criticising individuals for their differences
- making assumptions about people's differences
- excluding people from activities because of their differences
- avoiding people because they are different
- negative body language towards people who are different.

One of the fundamental principles of caring is that individuals are treated fairly, justly and without any form of discrimination – as outlined in the *Code of Practice for Social Care Workers* (GSCC, 2002a). Indeed, it encourages care workers to:

1. acknowledge diversity
2. promote anti-discriminatory practice
3. challenge any behaviour that might *stereotype* or label *individuals*.

The words and expressions that are used to convey everyday meanings are important as they can convey negative images of individuals and/or groups, for example, people who have a disability are often called 'handicapped'. This can lead to an assumption that disabled people are damaged versions of 'normal' people. Similarly, some phrases, such as 'old geezer', often convey a negative view of older people. As a care worker you should:

- avoid making stereotypical judgements about the potential ability of individuals
- encourage individuals to be confident in their abilities
- avoid encouraging service users to become overly dependent
- refuse to accept behaviour that is potentially discriminatory
- not participate in racist or sexist jokes, or participate in humour that pokes fun at individuals who have a disability.

Carers need to ensure that their colleagues also behave in ways that respect the rights and individuality of service users. With this point in mind, care workers need to set an example and make it clear that the following behaviours are unacceptable in a care environment:

- speaking in a derogatory way to individuals
- being rude to individuals
- undermining people's confidence
- talking down to individuals

- ignoring an individual's right to choose
- ridiculing an individual's values and beliefs
- not respecting an individual's culture.

Should this type of behaviour occur, it is vital that abuse and exploitation is identified and reported. Care workers should be trained to be aware of all forms of potential abuse and exploitation, and should know exactly what to do and who to go to if they have any suspicions or concerns. This will include a need to support whistle-blowing. Very often, staff can feel intimidated by abusers, especially if the abuser is a member of senior staff. There is often also a pressure to stick together with colleagues and many are tempted to keep quiet and ignore the abusive activity. It is especially important that care workers should be in no doubt that they will be supported if they take the step of reporting abuse and that to keep quiet about an abusive situation may in itself constitute a disciplinary or even criminal act.

REMEMBER...

- Older people who are dependent on others for their care needs are vulnerable to abuse and exploitation.

- Abuse often arises as a result of an imbalance of power between the service user and care giver.

- Older people may suffer from a number of different types of abuse, neglect and exploitation. These might include physical, sexual, financial or emotional.

- Be aware of the possible signs and symptoms of abuse.

- Always follow the policies and procedures of your care home when responding to any concerns about abuse, neglect or exploitation.

- Any concerns regarding suspected or alleged abuse or neglect must be reported to a supervisor or senior manager immediately.

- The issue of service user consent is key to any investigation of alleged abuse or exploitation. Therefore, care workers must ensure that allegations of abuse or exploitation are handled sensitively and in a confidential manner.

Finally, the activity on the next page is intended to 'test' your learning. It is not intended to catch you out in any way; rather, it gives you and your mentor an opportunity to discuss and find out where your particular strengths lie, and where you might need some additional help or support.

☺ Activity 36: Responding to abuse and neglect

Thomas is 86 years old and you are caring for him in his home where he lives with his son and daughter-in-law. He has recently suffered a stroke, which has affected his mobility and speech. You suspect that Thomas is being neglected, and might have been physically abused.

1. Identify physical signs that might suggest that Thomas is being abused.

2. Identify signs that might suggest that Thomas is being neglected.

3. Identify changes in Thomas' behaviour that led you to suspect abuse.

4. Identify factors that might make Thomas vulnerable to abuse or neglect.

5. What action should you take concerning your suspicions?

6. Where would you find information and advice concerning the protection of vulnerable adults?

7. What do the General Social Care Council codes of practice say about whistle-blowing?

Discuss your answers with your mentor, and then place them in your personal portfolio.

💡 Test your knowledge

RECOGNISE AND RESPOND TO ABUSE AND NEGLECT

The following questions are intended to 'test' your learning. They are not intended to catch you out in any way; rather, they give you an opportunity to review what you have learned, and to revisit and/or revise key parts of this chapter.

1. Give three measures outlined within the *No Secrets* report.

2. What does POVA stand for?

3. List three factors that are known to contribute to abuse and exploitation.

4. What are the six main types of abuse?

5. List three signs and symptoms of physical abuse.

6. List three signs of emotional abuse.

7. What is the Mental Capacity Act?

8. What is whistle-blowing?

9. What is the main priority when dealing with suspected abuse?

10. List three ways in which the privacy and dignity of service users can be respected.

Please refer to the answers in **Appendix one** (p119).

You have now completed the last chapter. Please ensure that you and your mentor complete the induction record on the next page, and that you place the answers to the learning activities in your **portfolio**.

When the induction record has been completed, place it in your **portfolio**, together with your **induction plan** and the answers to each of the **learning activities** you have completed.

CONGRATULATIONS!

✍ You have now completed your induction programme. Please ensure that you and your supervisor, or mentor, complete the induction record on the next page.

When the induction record has been completed, place it in your portfolio, together with the other induction plans you have completed.

☺ Your portfolio should also include the answers to each of the learning activities you have completed.

When completed, your portfolio will provide a permanent record of the competencies you have achieved during your induction. These can be used for accreditation of prior learning (APL) against an NVQ, or as a record for future employers.

We wish you every success in your new career.

Malcolm Day, Elaine Grade and Elaine Wilson

✍ My induction record

© Malcolm Day 2005

1. Name of domiciliary care worker ....

2. Name of manager/supervisor ....

3. Name of employer ....

4. Induction start date ....

5. Expected date of induction completion ....

6. This is to confirm that .... (name of care worker)
    has satisfactorily completed all of the learning activities related to:

Standard 5.0 Recognise and respond to abuse and neglect
     5.1 Legislation, policies and procedures
     5.2 Understand the nature of abuse and neglect
     5.3 Recognise the signs and symptoms of abuse and neglect
     5.4 Understand how to respond to suspected abuse or neglect
     5.5 Whistle-blowing.

7. Any comments from care worker/supervisor or mentor?

Signed (domiciliary care worker): .... Date: ....

Signed (supervisor/mentor): .... Date: ....

References

Barnes J (2006) *Making Referrals to the Protection of Vulnerable Adults (POVA) List.* Bristol: The Policy Press.

CSCI (2005) *Care Homes for Older People: National minimum standards.* London: CSCI.

Department for Constitutional Affairs (2007) *Mental Capacity Act: Code of practice.* London: The Stationery Office.

Department of Health (1995) *The Caldicott Committee. Report on the review of Patient-Identifiable Information.* London: The Stationery Office.

Department of Health (2000) *No Secrets: The protection of vulnerable adults. Guidance on the development and implementation of multi-agency policies and procedures.* London: The Stationery Office.

Department of Health (2002a) *Supported Housing and Care Homes – Guidance on regulation.* London: Department of Health.

Department of Health (2002b) *Care Homes for Older People National Minimum Standards.* London: The Stationery Office.

Department of Health (2003) *Domiciliary Care: National minimum standards – regulations.* London: Department of Health.

Egan G (1975) *The Skilled Helper.* California: Brooks/Cole.

General Social Care Council (2002a) *Code of Practice for Social Care Workers.* London: GSCC.

General Social Care Council (2002b) *Code of Practice for Employers of Social Care Workers.* London: GSCC.

Health and Safety Executive (1995) *Reporting of Injuries, Diseases and Dangerous Occurrences Regulations.* London: The Stationery Office.

Health and Safety Executive (2001) *Health and Safety in Care Homes.* London: HMSO.

Health and Safety Executive (2002) *Control of Substances Hazardous to Health Regulations.* London: The Stationery Office.

Ironbar NO (2002) *A Pathway to NVQs in Care: An underpinning knowledge.* Bath: Mark Allen Publishing.

Skills for Care (2005) *Common Induction Standards.* Available from: http://www.skillsforcare.org.uk/view.asp?id=751 [accessed February 2008].

The Stationery Office (2002) *The Domiciliary Care Agencies Regulations 2002.* London: The Stationery Office.

Further reading

Cooper J (2002) *The Care Homes Legal Handbook.* London: Jessica Kingsley Publishers.

Day M (2002) *Assessment of Prior Learning.* Cheltenham: Nelson Thornes.

Department of Health (2003) *Confidentiality. NHS code of practice.* London: The Stationery Office.

Nolan Y (2003) *Care NVQ Level 2.* London: Heinemann.

Walsh M (2005) *Health and Social Care NVQ 2 Candidate Handbook.* Cheltenham: Nelson Thornes.

Useful websites

Care Standards Commission Inspectorate: www.csci.org.uk

Department of Health: www.dh.gov.uk

General Social Care Council: www.gscc.org.uk

Skills for Care: www.skillsforcare.org.uk

Suzy Lamplugh Trust: www.suzylamplugh.org

UK Resuscitation Council: www.resus.org.uk

Appendix one

Answers to knowledge tests

CHAPTER ONE: THE PRINCIPLES OF CARING

1. **P:** respecting privacy
    R: respecting the rights of individuals
    I: recognising individuality
    C: working collaboratively with individuals and enabling them to make choices
    I: encouraging independence
    D: preserving dignity

2. Prejudices are the ideas and beliefs that we have about people and that may cause us to judge them before we get to know them properly.

3. Discrimination occurs when we treat others unfairly because of their appearance or beliefs.

4. The Sex Discrimination Act – men and women have equal rights to employment, services and facilities; the Race Relations Act – all forms of racial discrimination are prohibited; the Disability Discrimination Act – a disabled person must not be treated less favourably than someone who is able bodied.

5. Care plans; case notes; medical records; observation charts; prescription charts.

6. Assessment; planning; implementation; evaluation.

7. An overwhelming and uncontrollable need to void urine because of weakness of the muscles in and around the bladder.

8. Limbs may become contracted and muscles may become wasted if they are not exercised.

9. Chemicals from urine and faeces; pressure on the skin; friction.

10. By using the Waterlow Scale. The Waterlow Scale assesses the risk of skin breaking down by examining different aspects of a service user's life, such as weight, continence, skin type, mobility, sex, age, appetite, health status and any medications they are taking. This produces a numerical score that indicates whether the service user has a low, high or very high risk of developing pressure sores.

CHAPTER TWO: THE ROLE OF THE WORKER

1. A policy is an official document that gives information about what must be done in your care home. It sets out the standards that you must achieve in your work, and gives a clear indication of your responsibilities in relation to them.

2. A procedure is a document that explains how you should do your job, ie. it translates policies into working practice. Procedures are based on workplace values and principles to ensure that the job is done properly.

3. COSHH: Control of Substances Hazardous to Health Regulations.

4. RIDDOR: Reporting of Injuries, Diseases and Dangerous Occurrences Regulations.

5. High levels of absenteeism, lack of concentration and illnesses such as headaches.

6. According to the *Domiciliary Care: National minimum standards – regulations* (DoH, 2003), workers should receive formal supervision at least every three months.

7. Appraisal is a mechanism that allows you and your manager to discuss, openly and frankly, any issues relating to your performance at work. It is not part of the disciplinary process.

8. Mentorship is an informal arrangement and is usually provided by an experienced and trusted person from the care team eg. a senior care worker who is not part of the formal supervisory process.

9. National Vocational Qualification.

10. Encouraging good practice; maintaining the health and safety of staff, service users and their families; obeying the law.

CHAPTER THREE: MAINTAINING HEALTH AND SAFETY AT WORK

1. Protect the health and safety of staff, service users and visitors; draw up safety policies and procedures; make arrangements for policies and procedures to be carried out.

2. Vertebrae.

3. You should assess:
   a) task
   b) load
   c) environment
   d) individual capability.

4. **D**anger
   Response
   Airway
   Breathing.

5. Direct contact; indirect contact; inhalation; ingestion; injection.

6. Wear protective clothing; keep your nails clean and short; keep your hair tied back or covered; cover any minor wounds with a coloured waterproof dressing; do not smoke.

7. The clinical waste bin.

8. They are returned to the pharmacy.

9. Cleanse, apply a sterile dressing, apply pressure and elevate to control bleeding.

10. Place under cold running water for 10 minutes, apply sterile non-stick dressing and seek medical aid if necessary.

CHAPTER FOUR: COMMUNICATING EFFECTIVELY

1. To give information; to obtain information; to meet emotional needs; to exchange ideas; to meet social needs; to meet physical needs.

2. About 10% of our communication is spoken.

3. **S: sitting** squarely and opposite
   O: having an **open** posture
   L: leaning slightly towards the individual
   E: eye contact
   R: relax and show that you are listening

4. Facial expression; eye contact; posture; gesture; touch; proximity; tone of voice.

5. Closed questions; open questions; process questions; clarification.

6. Anger; denial; withdrawal; acceptance.

7. The Data Protection Act (1998) sets standards governing the storage and processing of personal data held in manual records and on computers. The Act works in two ways: it gives individuals (data subjects) certain rights, while requiring those who record and use personal information (data controllers) to be open about their use of that information and to follow sound and proper practices (the data protection principles).

8. You must: justify a purpose for recording and using service user information; only record and use information when it is absolutely necessary; use only the minimum information required; only access information on a strict 'need to know' basis; be aware of responsibilities concerning the recording and use of service-user information; understand and comply with the law eg. the Data Protection Act (1998).

9. Care records must be legible, factual, signed and dated and kept in a safe place; they must be tracked in a daily log book; daily log books should be returned to the service provider's office once full and when the care has finished; care records must be stored securely in the office and arranged so that the record can be found easily if needed urgently; care records should be stored closed when not in use, so that contents are not seen accidentally; care records should be held in secure storage, and marked confidential; there should restricted access to care records; there should be a secure means of destruction eg. shredding.

10. Always log-out of any computer system or application when work on it is finished; do not leave a terminal unattended and logged-in; do not share log-ins with other people; do not reveal passwords; avoid using short passwords, or using names or words that are known to be associated; always clear the screen of a previous service user's information before seeing another; use a password-protected screen-saver to prevent casual viewing of confidential information by others.

CHAPTER FIVE: RECOGNISE AND RESPOND TO ABUSE AND NEGLECT

1. Social services are to have lead status for protecting vulnerable adults; social services to have a co-ordinating role in developing local policies and procedures for protecting vulnerable adults; all relevant agencies to work collaboratively and develop inter-agency policies and procedures.

2. POVA: Protection of Vulnerable Adults.

3. Prolonged stress among the caregivers or care workers; feelings of resentment and hostility towards the service user; deeply held prejudices and stereotypes towards the elderly; financial dependency on the service user by a child or spouse; unrestricted access to service user's finances by child or spouse; poor levels of practical competence in caring; inadequate monitoring or supervision of a carer or care worker.

4. Physical; emotional; financial; sexual; neglect; racial or cultural.

5. Unexplained bruises or cuts, especially where they reflect the shape of an object used, of a hand or of finger marks; loss of hair in clumps or abrasions on the scalp from hair-pulling; unexplained fractures; unexplained burns or scalding; delays in reporting injuries; vague, implausible or inappropriate explanations; multiple injuries or a history of past injuries, especially falls.

6. Fearfulness; mood changes, including depression, irritability and unhappiness; low self-esteem; changes in sleep and appetite patterns; withdrawn, self-isolating behaviour.

7. The Mental Capacity Act (2005) provides a statutory framework to empower and protect vulnerable people who are not able to make their own decisions. It makes it clear who can take decisions, in which situations, and how they should go about this. It enables people to plan ahead for a time when they may lose capacity. Guidance on the Act is provided in a Code of Practice for health and social care workers.

8. Whistle-blowing is the reporting (by a social care worker) of unsafe or discriminatory practice.

9. The main priority when dealing with suspected abuse is safety of yourself and the service user.

10. Personal care and support is provided in a way that maintains and respects privacy, dignity and the lifestyle of the person receiving care at all times; all care workers use the term of address preferred by the service user; all care workers are instructed during their induction on how to treat service users with respect; service users should be enabled to exercise their legal rights; service users must be safeguarded from abuse, exploitation and neglect; care workers are responsive to the race, culture, religion, age, disability, gender and sexuality of the person receiving care and their relatives and representatives.

Appendix two

Protection of Vulnerable Adults (adapted from Barnes, 2006)

The Protection of Vulnerable Adults (POVA) scheme was introduced in July 2004 as a recommendation of the Care Standards Act (2000). It aims to protect vulnerable adults aged 18 years and over in care settings in both England and Wales.

The POVA register is maintained by the Department for Children, Schools and Families on behalf of the Secretary of State for Health. The register consists of a list of people who are banned from working with vulnerable adults in registered care services in England and Wales. These people have been dismissed from care work because they have been found guilty of harming vulnerable adults and are judged to be unsuitable to work with any other social care users.

Employers are required to check the POVA register when recruiting workers, carers or volunteers in regular contact with vulnerable adults. They are also required to make a referral to the register whenever they have decided that, in their view, a worker, carer or volunteer is guilty of misconduct that has harmed or placed a vulnerable adult at risk of harm and when they have suspended, dismissed or moved that person to a non-care position.

When an individual's name is placed on the POVA list, that person is not able to work with vulnerable adults until their name is removed from the list. It is therefore an offence for people who are on the register to knowingly apply for, offer to do, accept or do any work in a paid or unpaid caring position. Anyone employing them will be in breach of regulations relating to fitness of staff.

The list covers care workers, including volunteers and adult placement carers, who are working with vulnerable adults aged 18 years or over in:

- registered care homes
- registered domiciliary care agencies
- registered adult placement schemes.

Officials in the POVA Team in Darlington review POVA referrals and make recommendations to the Secretary of State for Health, who takes the final decision about listing any individual. Referral does not automatically lead to listing.

A referral is usually made only when the employer's own disciplinary procedures have been concluded. Where the offence is very serious, a referral can be made after a worker or carer has been suspended, in which case they may be provisionally listed until the outcome is clear.

POVA referrals are quite separate from the employer's own disciplinary procedures, they flow from the process but do not influence it.

Further information

- Barnes J (2006) *Making Referrals to the Protection of Vulnerable Adults (POVA) List.* Bristol: The Policy Press.

- UNISON (2007) *Reported: A UNISON guide to handling POVA cases.* London: UNISON.

- The POVA team can be contacted on their telephone advice line: 01325 391328.

Appendix three

The Mental Capacity Act (2005)

The Mental Capacity Act (2005) provides a statutory framework to empower and protect vulnerable people who are not able to make their own decisions. It makes it clear who can take decisions, in which situations and how they should go about this. It enables people to plan ahead for a time when they may lose capacity. Guidance on the Act is provided in a *Code of Practice* for health and social care workers.

The Act is underpinned by a set of five key principles.

1. A presumption of capacity – every adult has the right to make their own decisions and must be assumed to have the capacity to do so unless it is proved otherwise.

2. The right for individuals to be supported to make their own decisions – people must be given all appropriate help before anyone concludes that they cannot make their own decisions.

3. Individuals must retain the right to make what might be seen as eccentric or unwise decisions.

4. Anything done for or on behalf of people without capacity must be in their best interests.

5. Anything done for or on behalf of people without capacity should be as least restrictive of their basic rights and freedoms as possible.

The Act deals with the assessment of a person's capacity and actions of carers of those who lack capacity.

- **Assessing lack of capacity:** the Act outlines a test for assessing whether a person lacks capacity to take a particular decision at a particular time. It is a 'decision-specific' test, ie. no one can be labelled 'incapable' as a result of a particular medical condition or diagnosis and a lack of capacity cannot be established merely by reference to a person's age, appearance, or any condition or aspect of a person's behaviour that might lead others to make unjustified assumptions about capacity.

- **Best interests:** everything that is done for, or on behalf of, a person who lacks capacity must be in that person's best interests. The Act provides a checklist of factors that decision-makers must work through when deciding what is in a person's best interests. A person can put his/her wishes and feelings into a written statement if they so wish, which the decision-maker must consider. Also, carers and family members gain a right to be consulted.

- **Restraint/deprivation of liberty:** section six of the Act defines restraint as the use or threat of force where an incapacitated person resists, and any restriction of liberty or movement whether or not the person resists. Restraint is only permitted if the person using it reasonably believes it is necessary to prevent harm to the incapacitated person, and if the restraint used is proportionate to the likelihood and seriousness of the harm.

The Act deals with two situations where a designated decision-maker can act on behalf of someone who lacks capacity.

- **Lasting powers of attorney (LPAs):** the Act allows a person to appoint an attorney to act on their behalf if they should lose capacity in the future. This is like the current enduring power of attorney (EPA), but the Act also allows people to let an attorney make health and welfare decisions.

- **Court appointed deputies:** the Act provides for a system of court appointed deputies to replace the current system of receivership in the Court of Protection. Deputies will be able to take decisions on welfare, healthcare and financial matters as authorised by the Court but will not be able to refuse consent to life-sustaining treatment. They will only be appointed if the Court cannot make a one-off decision to resolve the issues.

The Act creates two new public bodies to support the statutory framework, both of which will be designed around the needs of those who lack capacity.

- **A new Court of Protection:** the new Court will have jurisdiction relating to the whole Act and will be the final arbiter for capacity matters. It will have its own procedures and nominated judges.

- **A new Public Guardian:** the Public Guardian and their staff will be the registering authority for LPAs and deputies. They will supervise deputies appointed by the Court and provide information to help the Court make decisions. They will also work together with other agencies, such as the police and social services, to respond to any concerns raised about the way in which an attorney or deputy is operating. A Public Guardian Board will be appointed to scrutinise and review the way in which the Public Guardian discharges their functions. The Public Guardian will be required to produce an annual report about the discharge of their functions.

The Act also includes three further key provisions to protect vulnerable people.

- **Independent mental capacity advocate (IMCA):** an IMCA is someone appointed to support a person who lacks capacity but has no one to speak for them. The IMCA makes representations about the person's wishes, feelings, beliefs and values, at the same time as bringing to the attention of the decision-maker all factors that are relevant to the decision. The IMCA can challenge the decision-maker on behalf of the person lacking capacity if necessary.

- **Advance decisions to refuse treatment:** statutory rules with clear safeguards confirm that people may make a decision in advance to refuse treatment if they should lose capacity in the future. It is made clear in the Act that an advance decision will have no application to any treatment that a doctor considers necessary to sustain life unless strict formalities have been complied with. These formalities are that the decision must be in writing, signed and witnessed. In addition, there must be an expressed statement that the decision stands 'even if life is at risk'.

- **A criminal offence:** the Act introduces a new criminal offence of ill treatment or neglect of a person who lacks capacity. A person found guilty of such an offence may be liable to imprisonment for a term of up to five years.